ALL THE WAY FOR DOC

A memoir by Whitworth Stokes

Copyright © 2009 Whitworth Stokes

Whitworth Stokes
1500 Rufer Avenue
Louisville, KY 40204-1634
(502) 583-5217
whitstok@aol.com

ISBN: 978-0-557-64016-4

WEST END HIGH SCHOOL (1937-1968),
WEST END MIDDLE SCHOOL (1968-),
NASHVILLE, TENNESSEE.

TABLE OF CONTENTS

PHOTOS&ILLUSTRATIONS

Dedicated to Joe and Ruth Shapiro.

WESTEND HIGH SCHOOL

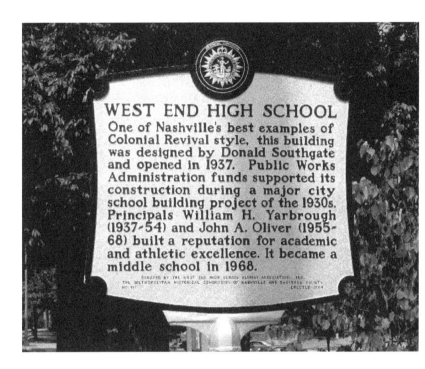

WEST END HIGH SCHOOL
One of Nashville's best examples of
Colonial Revival style, this building
was designed by Donald Southgate
and opened in 1937. Public Works
Administration funds supported its
construction during a major city
school building project of the 1930s.
Principals William H. Yarbrough
(1937-54) and John A. Oliver (1955-
68) built a reputation for academic
and athletic excellence. It became a
middle school in 1968.

It is July 26, 2008 and I am in Nashville, Tennessee on a hot humid Saturday afternoon and I have driven 175 miles this morning from Louisville, Kentucky where I live now. While it may be a typical summer day in the town of my birth, today is not a typical day at this location. I am visiting my old high school, West End High School, which is now West End Middle School. After extensive remodeling the school is preparing for the new school year which begins in less than a month. Today is an open house for former students to come and see what is new, as well as what might look the same as it did years ago. I am now seventy one years old and I am guessing the people in attendance will be well past fifty and some near eighty. This is confirmed later when I overhear names I recognize from long ago. The names are familiar because this school was a big part of my life when I was a child looking forward to being a West High Bluejay, just like my cousins and older brother. It continued to be a part of my life until I left Nashville in 1969.

I graduated in 1954 and went on to Vanderbilt University with many of my classmates who are now preparing for a 50th Reunion at that school. Vanderbilt graduates are called "Quinqs" when they reach the 50 year milestone. I am not sure how that custom came about, but I think it has something to do with Greek numbers and has been in use for so long that no one questions where it came from. West High graduates do not have any particular terminology to identify themselves. We are just people who "went to West."

The past tense is appropriate because the school I attended was an all white, legally segregated school near what was the western city limit at that time of the sleepy southern town of Nashville. The school today is an integrated inner city institution in the robust metropolis that calls itself "Music City, U.S.A." The faculty and student body today bears little resemblance to the school I attended. But, when you look for similarities instead of differences there is a lot that is familiar at the school I am walking into after being away for several years.

This is not the first time I have been back since graduation. I went to several football and basketball games between 1954 and 1969, but I only remember two or three times when I actually went inside the school. The first was at a twenty year reunion in 1974. The school was in the early stages of transition from a high school to a middle school as the population moved to the suburbs and baby boomers created a need for more of what were then called "junior highs." Actually West was both a high school and a junior high when I went there, but the grades 7-9 were small and in classrooms on the third floor of the building. In 1974 the school looked about the same as I remembered it and many of the faculty members were in attendance. Even though the racial composition of the school was experiencing drastic changes, the portrait of the original principal, Dr. W.H. Yarbrough (Doc) hung in the entrance hall. The trophy cases with all the Blue Jay victories in segregated athletics were in the same case that was there when I graduated twenty years earlier.

Thirty years later I went inside in 2004 for our 50th reunion and the school was a mess as the renovation process was about to begin in earnest. We were restricted to the lunchroom and auditorium. A dusty out of tune piano was wheeled in for the music that was part of a memorial service for deceased classmates. Only one faculty member who was alive was in attendance. The portrait of Doc was gone and the trophy cases appeared to house only middle school items. So as I enter the school on this humid Saturday I am not really sure what I am going to find, but I have been assured that a truce of sorts has been reached between the "old and the new."

The school opened in 1937 which was the same year I was born. It sits on a large lot well back from West End Avenue. West End is a continuation of a main street that starts at the west bank of the Cumberland River adjacent to Fort Nashborough and is called Broadway. At the top of one of Nashville's many hills the street splits. The left (or south) fork continues as Broad Street and the right (or north) fork continues as West End Avenue until it becomes Harding Road and eventually Highway 70 to Memphis. When I was growing up all traffic arriving from west of Nashville went right by the school which was so impressive from the road many thought it was the State Capitol! Interstate 40 reduced West End to an artery for city traffic, but the view is still impressive even to people who see it every day. Because of the large expanse of land (Elmington Park) in front of it, which comprises several acres, the building appears to be much larger than it is. Notwithstanding the impressive façade the front entrance is rarely used because all parking is behind the school and most people arrive by car. So it is today when I park in the small lot that used to house the few cars that students drove when I was in school. It occurs to me that might be another reason to change from a high school to a middle school. Most high school students today seem to own cars and there would be no place to put them.

When I get out of my car I run into a recognizable former student who was a year behind me and later married a former girl friend of mine. We chat as we near the side door of the school, passing a couple of vintage cars that are parked there. I recognize one as a 1957 Chevy because I actually owned one sometime in the 1960s. The other car is even older and I have no idea what it is, but I am not here to look at cars anyway so I move into the school. The first view is something of a shock because the hallway floor now has a bright tile pattern that looks out of place for a school built in the 1930s. The brick walls that used to house pictures of state basketball championship teams (1944, 1946, and 1948) are bare. As I approach the office the restoration/remodeling effort is less annoying. The entrance hall tile floor is original and there are three trophy cases. One is devoted to the basketball and other victories of the high school of my youth. Prominently displayed are the trophies of the 1954 state championship team I was almost a part of. That team was something of an improbable winner and was cheered on by the repetition of the cheer "All The Way For Doc." Dr. W.H. Yarbrough had been the principal of the school since it opened in 1937 and was scheduled to retire at the end of the school year. There is a quote from Dr. Martin Luther King, Jr. on the wall where Doc's picture used to hang. Doc's favorite quote was from a Sam Walter Foss poem, "let me live in a house by the side of the road and be a friend to man." The King quote is not so passive, but it is hardly the type of rhetoric that once struck so much fear in the minds of many people. They could have quoted Malcolm X or Stokley Carmichael if that was the goal. On the back wall inside the auditorium are large framed pictures of several all white graduating classes from the 1960s. This is obviously a custom that started after I left school because I do not recall ever seeing one until today. There are no similar pictures elsewhere in the school and the collection is certainly incomplete. It was a high school for over thirty years, so why do you just have a few from the final years of the school? It strikes me that someone took various mementos from the early years and put them on that wall because they didn't fit anywhere else.

If I had thought about it I would have looked at the curtain over the stage of the auditorium to see if it still had the mysterious "HH" at the top. The school was almost named after the Mayor Hilary Howse in 1937, but because it was a WPA New Deal project it could not be named for a living person. Notwithstanding that prohibition the school board actually did name the school for the Mayor hence the curtain was ordered. To put the matter to rest

Mayor Howse sent a letter to the board on November 10, 1937 declining the honor. The matter was resurrected when the Mayor died unexpectedly on January 2, 1938 and the school was renamed for a short period of time before protests from student and parent groups forced the school board to back down and West End High School was adopted as the official name of the school. However, the gymnasium was to be called the Hilary E. Howse Gymnasium, but if there was any plaque or other indication of that I don't recall ever seeing it.

The school has air conditioning now which was unheard of when I was a student. We didn't have it in our homes or our cars, much less a school. If you wanted to be cool you went to a movie or a drugstore. Today the front entrance hall is cool, but not as much as the rest of the school because one of the three double doors is propped open. A steady stream of visitors is going in and out of the door to look at the new veranda tiles at the front entranceway to the school. The original tiles were in terrible shape and as a fund raising device people were encouraged to buy a tile with whatever inscription they wanted to place on it. Looking at the over one hundred named squares provides a real history of the school back at a time when I was first exposed to the cheer "West is best, West is right, West is a chest of dynamite." The school won a state basketball championship in 1944 and there are tiles in memory of players from that team. The 1946 championship team is remembered with names like Billy Lawrence, a Viet Nam war hero, and later Superintendent of the Naval Academy at Annapolis, Maryland. 1948 is remembered by the family of Bob Dudley Smith who went on to play at Vanderbilt. He was never called Bob, Bobby, or even Robert. He was always Bob Dudley which is what people call him today. My 1954 class probably has more tiles than the three previous champions simply because we are not quite as old as the others. However, it isn't just athletes who are remembered. Teachers like Lucille Hines (chemistry and physics), Anna Dembsky (English), and Inez Alder (speech and drama) are mentioned several times. There are numerous references to Doc. To my surprise I find a tile with the name of the guy I met earlier in the parking lot. His wife is named with him even though they were divorced a few years before the tile naming project began. I assume it is just an acknowledgement of a happier and simpler time. No one from my family has a name to look at and I find myself feeling guilty about routinely shredding the notice I got a few years back inviting me to participate.

By this time I am beginning to experience a feeling that I cannot put into words, but something is telling me I need to walk every floor and hallway of this building today which is what I do for the next hour. Down the locker lined first floor hallway to the east end of the building I pass the classroom of Anne Battle who taught French and Spanish. I took Spanish for two years and do not remember any of it today. I took the course to meet the language requirement of colleges I was interested in attending. The lockers appear new and are painted a deep reddish color. They are still recessed into the walls and have combination locks on them. The lockers I recall were a drab metallic color and I don't remember if we locked them or not frankly. Next was the classroom of Anna Dembsky, a colorful English teacher whose wild animation actually distracted from the subject matter in my opinion. As a result I transferred to the classroom next door, Mrs. Ellis, in the spring. The move was met with scorn by Dembsky who had taught my cousins, Leslie and Kendall Cram, and my older brother Brock. But, it was a relief to me to get away from the daily drama. Another reason I wanted the change was to be in a different class from a girl friend after our breakup, but I didn't tell Doc that when I requested the transfer.

At the end of the hallway is the room where I took Latin for two years. I doubt if Latin has been taught in public high schools for decades, but I learned more about grammar in that room than I ever did in English class. Of course I also learned that "all Gaul is divided into three parts," which I haven't had much reason to use since I was in Mrs. Watkins class. She was nearing retirement and was thought of as old by her students, but she was probably several years younger than I am now. At the other end of the hallway was Mrs. Johnson's room. Annette Johnson was a young teacher starting out back then. West might have been her first job and I took her classes in English and geography. She was one of the few faculty members to attend our 50th reunion and she greeted me with the statement "you were so much trouble."

As I circle back to go to the other end of the first floor I am impressed with the remodeling effort at the school. New windows are everywhere and I am sure they are more energy efficient than the ones they replaced. I wonder if they even open. I once jumped out of an open window in Miss Battle's first floor classroom to retrieve a pencil that had been knocked out of my hand by a classmate. The teacher was writing on the blackboard at the time and I was back through the window before she turned around to see what people were laughing at. I don't suppose they use blackboards and chalk anymore either. When someone explained I had jumped out the window and back in she refused to believe it. It's not just the windows that are new. The hardwood floors have been sanded and refinished to a much more natural look than I remember. I am glad they kept the old floors. My children went to schools that had all weather carpeting that could withstand anything, but it was never very attractive.

Many of the classrooms appear to be for different subjects than the ones I took years ago. I realize there is a difference in a high school curriculum, circa 1954 and a middle school of today, but the subjects are unfamiliar. What is "earth science" anyway? Will the leaders of tomorrow be better off taking earth science instead of Latin? My feelings of nostalgia are beginning to be replaced with feelings of simply being old.

As I pass the school office I decide to see what it feels like to go in voluntarily, instead of being summoned for my latest transgression. I could almost see the school secretary, Miss Smith, sitting there and hear her say "Doc wants to see you." It wasn't always a disciplinary matter because my family had known Doc for years and sometimes he just wanted to talk. But, there were at least two instances where I was in there for something serious enough to deserve suspension, if not expulsion. For whatever reason he simply admonished me for my childish behavior and said he expected better from me. He was the principal at Peabody Demonstration School before West and my mother was one of his students there. Doc was on a first name basis with most of his students, although he often could not remember their names and just referred to them as "kiddies." Doc's problem with names wasn't restricted to students.

At an assembly program he once introduced the guest speaker Rabbi Silverman as "Father Silverman."

Doc was born May 1, 1884 in Athens, Alabama, but moved to Texas where he attended and taught school even though he had not acquired a degree until he enrolled in the University of Texas in his mid-thirties. He transferred to Vanderbilt in his final year and later received an M.A. and doctorate from Peabody College. He taught history and served as the Director of Peabody Demonstration School for fourteen years before moving to the new school on West End Avenue.

I pick up speed as I head down the hallway toward the stairs which will take me to the second floor. I pass classrooms that were used for the band and the choir and I never had any involvement with either activity. There was a room that was used to teach typing…noisy manual typewriters with a carriage return…but boys couldn't take the class. It was assumed we would be dictating letters to our secretaries! It looks like faculty members today are not doing any dictating because these first floor rooms now house copying machines and computer terminals for their use. There is even an elevator that has been added which I assume was an accessibility requirement. As I walk up the stairs I notice the original wooden handrails are still in place, but a sturdier metal handrail hovers above it now. Another concession to legal requirements I assume. The new rails are painted blue which is one of the school colors. The first year of the school's existence the school board designated the colors orange and white and the team was called the Orangemen. The first senior class had a large number of graduates who were going to enter Vanderbilt (Black and Gold) and a much smaller number headed to the University of Tennessee (Orange and White) and the Board's selection had not set well with them. In 1938 the colors of Blue and Grey were selected and the Blue Jay was adopted as a symbol, but that wasn't a simple matter. A school wide naming contest resulted in Westerners winning over Indians and Blue Streaks. However, local newspaper columnist "Red" O'Donnell had facetiously suggested Blue Jay because it "is one of the most unfriendly species of birds, always quarreling and stealing from its neighbors." For some reason the name stuck and now the color scheme appears throughout the building. I do not recall bright colors of any kind when I was in school. Maybe it's the windows and the floors, perhaps better lighting, but the whole place seems brighter than I recall.

A crowd has gathered at the first room on my left at the top of the stairs. It is called the Alumni Room and a number of grey haired people are pouring over old pictures and school newspapers. The pictures of white boys in short pants winning basketball championships which were once on the walls downstairs have found a new home, as well as the portrait of Doc. I spend some time there, not because I think I will discover anything new, but to immerse myself in things that remind me why I drove over three hours this morning. Actually a lot of the room is devoted to what happened at the school for many years after I left and I am reminded that John Oliver who followed Doc was principal for about the same length of time. Both names are on the plaque at the corner of West End and Bowling Avenues. In the period West End was a high school (1937-1968) there were only two principals. In the following years the school has had nine principals. From this one can assume that becoming a high school principal is a destination job whereas a middle school or junior high position is viewed as a stepping stone.

When Doc's successor was announced many people, including myself, thought it was going to be Dr. W. H. Oliver who was the principal at East Nashville High School at that time. Doc often simply signed his initials (WHY) so if Dr. Oliver did the same it would amount to replacing a "why" with a "who." The last name was correct, but we had the wrong Oliver. Dr. W.H. Oliver left East High in 1957 to become superintendent of schools. It was his brother, John Oliver, who became the second principal of West End High School.

Next door is the library which looks almost the same except for the computer terminals that are present there just as they are in all the other rooms. I look to my right and expect to see Billy Owens, an end on the football team and forward on the basketball team, sitting with his girl friend. They were usually there before school started just waiting for classes to begin. Because they were two years apart in school and did not have any classes together this was one of their few chances to talk which you were allowed to do in the library at that hour. It was a good thing I could find them at that spot every morning. My senior year I had taken my first report card home. My mother looked at it, but did not sign it. Back then the grade record keeping process was a completely manual paper copy affair. You were required to take the report card home, get it signed by a parent, and returned the following day. I got Billy's girl friend to sign it after I told her my mother's name was Lucy Brock Stokes. Well, six weeks later I took the same report card home and my mother wanted to know whose signature that was on the back. I explained and for the rest of the year the student signed the report card because my mother's signature would not look at all like hers. She and Billy broke up after he went away to college, but I saw her a few times after my senior year. I would jokingly refer to her as "mother."

I leave the library and continue down the second floor hallway to the stairs that lead to the third floor. By now the classrooms are beginning to take on a similarity, albeit a new and different sameness from an earlier time. Perhaps it's because I did not have many classes in these particular rooms or the unfamiliarity of the teacher's names on the doorways. I try to remember if there were teacher names identifying classrooms when I was a student, but I draw a blank. School starts in a few weeks and textbooks are stacked on desks in many of the rooms. I resist the temptation to take a peek at the books, but I do wonder if they are much better than the ones I had. They all look new and I don't remember anything but used books when I was in school. Many were out of date or certainly not current. I remember an American History class that stopped at the Great Depression. I was never sure if that was because the school board could not stand President Roosevelt and the New Deal, or because we were using textbooks printed before World War II.

I cut through the auditorium balcony on my way to the original gym. I call it original because a newer and larger one was added next to the school a few years after I left. The original gym is above the cafeteria and has a brick wall around the single basketball court. You do not have to go far out of bounds to get slammed into an unforgiving wall. The only protective mats were behind the goals. The backboards are wooden and painted white. There was no need for glass because all the seats are on the sides of the court above the brick wall. There was some concern whether a team that played in a gym with white backboards would have a visual problem at tournament time when they played on college courts (Lipscomb and Vanderbilt) with glass backboards. There never appeared to be any discernible difference which I attribute to the fact that all rims are ten feet off the ground and a good shooter is a good shooter wherever you put them. Most players grow up playing on outdoor courts that often have fan shaped backboards, loose rims, no nets, and whatever excuses an untalented player wants to use for missing a shot. I grew up shooting at a loose rim with a tattered net on the wall of a garage in our backyard. It was not close to ten feet above the ground since the garage wasn't that tall. Because the yard sloped shots were not the same height from one side of the yard to the other. Our large boxer dog Bill made the footing treacherous as well, but that's where I learned to shoot a basketball. When I got to West End and made the junior high team I thought the facilities were first rate. Well maybe not the small locker room which was under the stands on the south side of the gym. The junior high team practiced at 6:30 in the morning and throughout the day there were physical education classes, male and female, in the gym. After school varsity sports took over so the locker room was in continuous use with showers running all day every day. I remember it as loud, crowded and steamy.

The indescribable feelings return as I step out on the basketball court and feel transported back to my grammar school years when my father would take me and my brother to games. One time we had to stand on the narrow sideline almost under the goal because the seats were filled. The seating capacity of that gym was about the same as the enrollment of the school. I am not sure if the designers assumed no one outside the school would want to attend or if they figured only a few students would show up. It was probably the best they could come up with given the limited amount of money available to build a school as the country struggled to come out of the Great Depression. The football stadium behind the school was a visible reminder of that era because it had a plaque on it which identified it as a WPA project. I decide not to disturb my pleasant nostalgic mood by looking in the old locker room and I go down the stairs to the cafeteria.

The lunchroom was probably the right choice for a last stop. It bears little resemblance to what I remember. Bright colors abound which again include flooring unimaginable in 1937. I realize I have gotten what I came for and head to the parking lot. It appears the same "tire kickers" who were standing by the 1957 Chevy when I came in are still there. A handful of smokers has retreated to a shady area a short distance away. They cup their hands around the cigarettes as if they are protecting them from the wind, but there is no hint of a breeze on this day. Their furtive glances give the appearance of looking out for a faculty member who will report them for smoking on school property.

That night I went to dinner with a classmate from the 1954 class. I hadn't seen him since the reunion in 2004, but we stay in touch by email. When he asked me why I made the trip to school I have to admit that I am toying with writing a book about the basketball championship team. Going to the school was just part of the research along with several pages of newspaper clippings I have gathered on earlier trips. The back issues of both daily papers (Tennessean and Banner) are on microfilm at the Nashville Public Library and I also have a scrapbook that I put together in 1954. Maybe I had a premonition that something was going to happen because I started keeping the daily news stories when the tournament began. West had already shown they were a good team that year with only three losses, but no one thought they would go beyond the District tournament if they got that far. But I had all the stories, programs, and even ticket stubs from the start to the surprising finish three weeks later when West End High School won its fourth state title, the most for any school in the state at that time.

My dinner companion encourages me to write the book. He was not an athlete. He played Hamlet in a school play his junior year and the following summer we worked together in Lake Wales, Florida on an outdoor drama about the Seminole Indians. The idea of a book appealed to him because of the dramatic aspects of the era that was about to change drastically. We won the championship on March 13, 1954. On May 17, 1954 the United States Supreme Court declared segregation on the basis of race in the public schools unconstitutional. That same year Nera White graduated from high school in Lafayette, Tennessee and moved to Nashville to set records in AAU basketball for the next fifteen years while playing for Nashville Business College. NBC was already an international powerhouse in women's basketball before Nera arrived. Across town from the Vanderbilt gymnasium where the state high school basketball tournament was played the National Negro High School basketball tournament was held at Tennessee A & I (now Tennessee State University) for the 25th consecutive year. Laurinburg Institute (NC) defeated Dunbar High from Somerset, Kentucky 70-58. West beat Lafollette by a much lower score 42-40 in their final game. Local papers covered the West High victory as a front page story. High school sports were usually the lead stories in the sports section of the Banner and Tennessean in my youth. AAU and "colored" basketball was rarely mentioned. If it was the story would be below the fold on an inside sports page. My friend was right. It was not the end of an era, but it certainly was the beginning of the end.

BASKETBALL

James Naismith is credited with designing the game of basketball in 1891 in Springfield, Massachusetts. He was said to be looking for an indoor sport that could be played at the YMCA during the winter months. The game first envisioned by Naismith hardly resembles the fast moving sport of today. The version that was played in Tennessee high schools in the 1940s and 1950s was somewhere between both extremes. Gone was the peach basket goals that held the ball after a made shot and a center jump was no longer required after each point. Nine players on a side were just too many. Some say that was because Dr. Naismith had eighteen people in his first class so he divided them into two equal teams. When West End High School opened in 1937 there were five on a side, but the idea of a shot clock or a three point shot was not on anyone's mind.

Tennessee probably grasped basketball later than states like Indiana and Kentucky where small town identity often evolved around the local high school team. Players at the state university were often the best players in their home state and it was considered treason to not go to a school like the University of Kentucky if you were a local boy unless Baron Adolph Rupp decided you were not good enough to play for the Big Blue. The biggest event in many towns was the high school basketball games played in a gym that was little more than an expanded barn. Hence the term "barnburner" was used to describe a particularly exciting game. It is still used today although the cavernous arenas of the late 20th century can hardly be called barns. In the movie Hoosiers Gene Hackman is supposedly enthused as he drives through the rural area where he has been hired to coach because he sees a basketball goal on the side of every garage and barn with kids playing. There will be no shortage of talent is his conclusion, but the scene in a major city even in 1950 would be similar with playgrounds adjacent to every park and school, as well as many back yards. Basketball is one of those sports, like golf, where you can actually practice the skills you need by yourself. Other sports like football, baseball, and tennis require others to either throw or hit a ball for you to hit or catch. But basketball is something you can spend long hours working on dribbling and shooting without a soul around.

What you do not learn by yourself unfortunately are those skills that define a winning team, particularly passing and defense. No need to set a screen when there's no one else on your team. On the playground you can play two on two and set a screen for your teammate and they may just look at you like you're crazy. Or you can yell "switch" if you're on defense and get the same reaction. There is a lot of raw talent on the playgrounds and backyards of America whether you're talking about 1944 or 2008, but it takes a coach to put it all together into a winning team.

When West End High School opened in 1937 the coach was James Farrell and while his teams were above average the country was so engrossed in the recovery from the Great Depression and the beginning of World War II it would have to be said that high school athletics were at best a diversion from more serious matters. In addition to coaching football and basketball Farrell taught Algebra and Latin his first two years at the school. His best year was the 1939-1940 season when the football team tied for the city league championship and the basketball team won the District tournament and one game in the Regional before losing to Springfield 20-24. His overall record in football was 27-14-4 and 69-32 in basketball when he left West in 1942 to become principal at Tarbox Junior High School. A year later he became headmaster at Montgomery Bell Academy (MBA) and was then drafted in the Army. He was commissioned and became a pilot in the Army Air Corps stationed in the Pacific where he commanded the 140th Long Range Bomber Squadron.

He was followed by Tennessee Tech graduate Emmett Strickland who had been a high school teammate with future Alabama star Dixie Howell. At TPI, as the school was called then Strickland earned letters in football, basketball, and baseball. His coaching career began in Oneida, Tennessee in 1936 where his football team only lost one game. He moved to Nashville and coached for two years at Donelson. In 1939 he was assigned as a teacher at Cohn High School, but also served as the basketball coach at Hume-Fogg. This unusual arrangement continued in 1941 when he was transferred as a teacher to Howard High School. In 1942 he replaced James Farrell at West and resumed his career as a fulltime coach.

In basketball Strickland had an ability to assemble a diverse group of teenagers and mold them into a cohesive unit. Some of the players were truly talented and went on to play in college, but only Billy Joe Adcock (Vanderbilt 1947-1950) had an outstanding career. Some of the other players were frankly average, but they bought into Strickland's ideas about unselfish team play. It is true there were not that many schools to play against at that time and West was blessed to have families in the area that sent more than one son to play for the Bluejays. But, Strickland's record in the state tournament has never been surpassed. Between 1944 and 1948 his teams won the championship three times (1944, 1946, and 1948). The other years they either lost in the finals (1947) or won a consolation game for third place (1945). What makes this all the more remarkable is that Strickland was also the football coach so he couldn't start practicing basketball until that season was over which was often a matter of a few days between the end of one season and the start of another. Of course many of his players were involved in more than one sport and made the quick transition along with their coach, swapping cleats for sneakers.

The state basketball tournament in the 1940s was a compressed affair which meant playing as many as three games in less than 48 hours on the final weekend. But, then baseball practice would start immediately after the basketball tournament and the coach and players would be back on the field again swapping sneakers for spikes. In addition to these multiple coaching duties the coach (terms like athletic director were unheard of then) was expected to teach several physical education classes and maybe driver education as well. Somewhere in that busy day he would see that the laundry was done and clean practice equipment laid out. He might have one assistant for football, but none for basketball because there was also a junior high team at the school and a "B" team as well. The term junior varsity came along much later in Tennessee, but apparently it was already being used in the basketball leagues in Illinois and Indiana.

I discovered that when I started doing research for this book. My original intent was to write about the 1954 team, but it would be impossible to do so without touching on the entire history of the school. Also to my knowledge no one had actually written a book about that 1954 team, or any of the others. However, there were a lot of articles on the subject. Most treated it as a heroic effort against improbable odds by an undersized bunch of overachievers. This I discovered was the accepted way to treat such events and it seems that Illinois, Indiana, and Kentucky all have similar stories to tell about giant killers that won state tournaments in the 1950s. While this makes for interesting reading it is not necessarily accurate as history.

In Kentucky much is made of the team from tiny Cuba, Kentucky that won in 1952 against a much larger school from Louisville. The story loses a little of its novelty when you learn that 1952 was the second consecutive year that Cuba made it to the finals. The book about the Cuba Cubs, When Cuba Conquered Kentucky, captures the human side of the drama and is really more of a sociological analysis of small town life than a basketball story. Some critics have indicated the book could have used a ghost writer to help with the technical aspects of the game, but I found the specifics of their criticism to be petty. A book with an irritating tone of exaggeration, Once There Were Giants, describes the team from Hebron, Illinois who won in 1952. While it is true that Hebron is a very small town almost on the Wisconsin border, the school had been a basketball powerhouse for many years and the championship team had seven players who went on to play in college. I started reading a book about Milan, Indiana who won in 1954, but was not motivated to finish it because I was not convinced it was in fact The Greatest Basketball Story Ever Told, as the title proclaimed. I have no doubt there are people who believe that to be true and frankly will have no interest in the book I am writing.

The closest thing to the David vs. Goliath story in Tennessee is probably what happened immediately after 1954 when Linden, a truly small school from Perry County won the state title for the next three years. That was the subject of an excellent book, "Boys In Black," by Gene Pearce. One of the conclusions I reached in reading about these teams from small towns is that they had a distinct advantage over a city school in advance scouting of available talent. The schools in question in Illinois, Indiana, Kentucky, and Perry

County, Tennessee were usually the only school in the county as well as the primary source of entertainment for their community. It was easy to spot a player with potential, or at least height, very early in a place where everyone knows each other.

West High drew from three, originally four, junior high schools in an area of the city that had a wide range of household incomes. Closest to downtown was a school with the unlikely name of Tarbox. There was a John Tarbox who was a 19th century congressman from Massachusetts who had several schools named after him in that area, but what connection he had, if any, to the Nashville school of my youth is unknown. Tarbox was phased out of existence by the time I got to West, but I did see my brother play a junior high game there the year before it closed. It had to have the smallest gym I ever saw. It was little more than two classrooms put together with basketball goals at both ends. It was more similar to our backyard than a gymnasium, except you didn't have to worry about stepping into something the dog had deposited. The school building was demolished a long time ago for the unrelenting expansion of Music Row.

The easternmost part of the school zone was next to a combination of industrial development and public housing. Those students went to Waverly-Belmont which was named for the two neighborhoods of the city it covered. There was an overlap with the black community; both in segregated public housing and minority home ownership, and those students went to Cameron, one of three Negro high schools in the city. Waverly-Belmont was too far from West End High for students to walk so the school board paid for several city buses to pick up the students and take them back in the afternoon. This probably contributed to a severe limitation when it came to after school activities, but there were three players on the 1954 team (Billy Owens, Eddie Greer, and Bobby Glenn) from that school. The income level and incidence of home ownership was certainly higher than Tarbox, but probably not as high as the next feeder school moving westward.

Cavert Junior High was a perennial basketball powerhouse largely because of their excellent coach, Charles Malin. Cavert also had a high degree of support from parents and friends in the neighborhood which made it stand out from other schools in the junior high league. Basketball was a serious business at Cavert and a lot of players from there went on to play at West, including six on the 1954 team (Vaughn DuBose, Jimmy French, Archie Grant, Jerry Morrison, Buddy Parsons, and John Stephens). The history of Cavert is easier to ascertain than the other schools in the area. The school opened in 1928 and was named for a Nashville physician, Dr. A.J. Cavert, who was Assistant Superintendent of Schools in the late 1800s. The tiny gym, where Jimmy French made my life miserable in a junior high game in 1950, was replaced in 1964.

The final feeder school was West Junior High tucked away on the third floor of the school building and a perennial loser in basketball, although it drew from the most affluent area in the school zone and probably the most affluent area in the city limits at that time. Basketball was the only sport the baby Bluejays played and it was irrelevant to the school and its supporters, in contrast to the other junior highs where sports teams did not have to play second fiddle to an older squad. It might have also been embarrassing to have a team so bad at the same address as a high school that had a trophy case full of triumphs. The team I played on in 1950-1951 only won one game, or so we thought. After the game a discrepancy was discovered between the scoreboard and the official scorebook which showed the game ended in a tie and should have gone into overtime!

Notwithstanding that West Junior High did contribute a player to the state championship team, Eddie Gaines. Gaines was what was considered tall at that time, being all of 6' 3". There is a saying "you can't coach speed and you can't coach height" so any one that size in the early 1950s would get a chance to make most teams. Actually Eddie was more than tall and a major contributor to the team. He shared duties with Butch Stephens at center which was a necessity because both had a tendency to get in foul trouble. Eddie was also on my junior high team that was credited with winning one game. They improved the next year and won two. Needless to say he did not come down from the third floor at West High with the winning attitude that the Cavert kids brought to the school.

The final member of the 1954 squad actually went to Howard Junior High outside the school district. Howard was close to the west bank of the Cumberland River and practically downtown.

Ralph Greenbaum was allowed to transfer to West so he could take Latin which was not offered at Howard High School. The high school was in a separate building next door to the junior high. Greenbaum's family eventually moved into the West End school zone a half block from the school, but his academic reason for transferring was serious. He was admitted to Yale after his senior year and after two years transferred to Vanderbilt. He then went to medical school and has been a practicing physician in Nashville for many years.

The record of West End High School in the first half of the 20th century is indeed impressive and it is not my intention to diminish it. But, it is certainly a reflection of the time that during the same period a "colored" school, Pearl High, participated in a national tournament eleven times before 1954. This pattern continued until the integration of the two school systems into one state tournament in basketball in 1965 and Pearl won that three times (1965, 1966, and 1981). Pearl High also won the girls state championship in 1980. In 1986 the school was phased out and merged with Cohn, a formerly white school.

During that same period AAU women's teams from Nashville, Vultee Bomberettes and Cook's Goldblumes, won five national titles. After 1958 the Nera White led team won the title ten more times in twelve years. Robert Ikard, a Nashville physician and Vanderbilt classmate of mine, wrote an excellent book, "Just For Fun, The Story of AAU basketball," that gives a full account of this neglected part of sports history. Legal changes led to the growth of women's basketball in college and the demise of the AAU in the last half of the 20th century, just as school integration led to the end of all black and all white teams.

THE STRICKLAND YEARS

On March 18, 1944 the country was still engaged in World War II. The day West End High School won the first of their four state basketball championships the front section of the Nashville papers carried these headline stories: "Allied Troops Clear Cassino in Northern Italy;" "Russians Move Into Rumania;" and "U.S. Bomb Kurile Islands, 960 Miles from Tokyo." On the domestic front a Senate committee approved what would become known as the G.I. Bill of Rights spelling out a wide range of benefits for the returning soldiers and sailors from a war that now appeared winnable. Local stores Cain Sloan, Castners, and Lovemans ran full page ads for upcoming Easter sales. But, the biggest ads were from Harveys, the new kid on the block. Fred Harvey had moved into the old Lebeck Building on Church Street and his liberal credit policies and promotions were beginning to change the way stores did business in ways that had many Nashvillians shaking their heads.

West entered the tournament with an impressive 28-2 season record. The games were held in the East Nashville High School gym which was hardly bigger than the small gym at West High. It had an unusual configuration and served as an auditorium so the basketball court was actually above many of the seated patrons. There were a limited number of seats around and above the stage, but that area was mostly for the teams and cheerleaders. In the opening game they defeated Peabody 39-32. This was not the local school affiliated with Peabody College where I would become a third grader in the fall, but a school with the same name from Trenton, Tennessee. To reach the finals they then beat Friendsville 37-31 and Elizabethtown was their last victim 38-30. No attendance figures were released and the news stories were quick to point out this was the first time a Nashville team had won in 17 years. The high scorer for the game was Eddie Lawrence, the first of the Lawrence brothers to play for West. Another member of the team was George Kelley who later had the distinction of playing football for the University of Tennessee and then basketball at Vanderbilt with a stint in the military sandwiched in between. The format for the tournament was certainly different from today with eight teams invited from different regions of the state. Through a series of games all eight teams finished with a trophy of some kind from first to eighth. It must have seemed cruel to allow a team to travel to the games and then go home after one loss. The number of games, and loss of prestige, appears to have had an effect as the scores on the final day were as low as the championship game. Chattanooga Southside beat Friendsville 37-34. Fifth position went to Nashville Hillsboro defeating Unionville 39-30. Seventh went to Peabody over Lawrenceburg 28-24.

On that same day the sport section carried a story under the headline "Rule Changes Would Aid Girls Basketball." Certainly the sport as played by men has undergone a large number of rule changes, but they pale by comparison to the changing status of the women's game. Women were initially playing on six person teams, but only three could be in each half of the court in what amounted to a three on three half court game. When the ball changed hands the guards who had been on defense now became dribblers who tried to move the ball to their forwards usually found standing at the center line. Their mobility was further limited by restrictions on the number of dribbles a player could take as well. One of the rule changes proposed allowed for a single player to be a rover and allowed to cross the center line. This rule was already used by the AAU and made for a faster paced game than the schools were playing. Unlimited dribbling was also a proposed change. However it would be years before the male and female versions, i.e., five on five, would become the standard. Even today there are some holdovers from the old rules, e.g., no ten second rule in the women's game.

There was no National Negro High School tournament in 1943 and 1944, but in 1945 the games moved to the Tennessee A & I campus where it remained until it was discontinued in 1964. During that period Nashville Pearl High competed with teams from many states, not just ones from the segregated Southern ones.

In 1946 the state tournament was held in Murfreesboro on the campus of what is now called Middle Tennessee State University (MTSU). Then it was the Middle Tennessee State Teachers College, but it had a facility that could accommodate the anticipated crowds of 1,200 fans. The Second World War was over and the country was returning to a peace time economy without the rationing of food and gas that had been imposed during the war. This did not assure harmony on the domestic front as the Democratic Party struggled to deal with the split between northern liberals and southern conservatives. The increased responsibilities that women and Negroes had assumed during the period of military conflict made them restless for a continuation of their new found status. It seems Rosie the Riveter was not going back to the kitchen without putting up a fight. A Negro baseball player, Jackie Robinson, was going to play for the Brooklyn Dodgers farm team in Montreal, Canada. If he was successful there the team intended to move him up to the major league team the following year. The armed services had been segregated during the war, although that was difficult to achieve in the Navy because of limited space on a ship. Now the military, with the blessing of President Truman was moving to full integration which was substantially completed by 1954.

West High entered the tournament with a record of 32-2 and the Bluejays were favored to win after failing to do so the previous year. They actually made it look easy by defeating Friendsville 34-32, McMinnville 45-19, and Livingston in the finals by a score of 50-32. The high scorer was Billy Joe Adcock with 21 points. Adcock went on to Vanderbilt where he received the first basketball scholarship ever offered by the school. Adcock actually played three sports at West (football, basketball, and baseball) the three years he was at the school. At Vanderbilt he played baseball and basketball, leading all scorers in the Southeastern conference in 1947-48 with a 17.1 average, 13th best in the nation. He was a consensus All-American his senior year and drafted by the Minneapolis Lakers. Instead of pro basketball he chose an engineering career having graduated with a 3.1 GPA. In 2002 he was inducted into the Tennessee Sports Hall of Fame.

It must have been academics that drew Adcock to Vanderbilt or maybe he wanted to be present at the start of a major change at the school which was about a mile closer to town on West End Avenue. After the war ended the basketball coach was an assistant football coach and no players were on athletic scholarships. The team practiced in a small gymnasium they shared with physical education classes. When I was in school later it was used for registration and little else. It became an art gallery and is on the National Register of Historic Buildings. Today it does not look like a place where basketball was ever played.

The Commodores played at a variety of places, including the unique East High facility where the 1944 state tournament was held. The closest locations to the campus were either Father Ryan High School or the Hippodrome, a skating rink which featured wrestling matches more than basketball. Both were within easy walking distance of the school, but have long since been demolished. They also played further away from the school in a building called the Classification Center. It was part of a military facility used to classify draftees and volunteers during the war and declassify or discharge them after the war. The small gym might have been an afterthought to provide some place for recreation for the troops. In 1946 we went to a game there which was a one sided affair against the nationally ranked Kentucky Wildcats. They were automatic SEC champions every year and later that year would win the NIT championship for the first time. UK would win one more NIT championship and seven NCAA tournament finals. But, that was all in the future. My father wanted my brother and me to see how the game should be played so in 1946 I saw my first college basketball game which Kentucky won easily by a score of 80-30. Later that year Vanderbilt played UK again in the Southeastern Conference tournament in Louisville, Kentucky and the score was even more lopsided, 98-29. The powers that be had seen enough. A full time coach was hired, scholarships were offered, and plans made for an on campus basketball arena. Bob Polk was an assistant coach at Georgia Tech and became the Commodore's first full time coach. He was a native of Tell City, Indiana and began to recruit in the basketball rich areas of Indiana and Kentucky. His eight year winning percentage (60.5%) is the second highest in the modern history of the school. As the first scholarship player and captain Adcock's teams showed improvement each year. In 1951, four years after the lopsided loss, Vanderbilt beat Kentucky in the SEC tournament 61-57. Adcock had graduated the year before, but there were two West players on that team, George Kelley, 1944, and Bob Dudley Smith, a star on the 1948 squad. A large building next to the football stadium was taking shape with Memorial Gymnasium scheduled to open in 1952.

In 1946 the state tournament was still an eight team affair with four games played on the final day to determine the final rankings. Soddy-Daisy beat McMinnville 39-32, Covington beat Jackson 35-31, and Fayetteville beat Friendsville 40-22. When West won in 1944 it ended seventeen years of East Tennessee domination. In 1946 the teams from East Tennessee were third place Soddy-Daisy, a combined school between the communities of Soddy and Daisy outside Chattanooga, and Friendsville who finished last. West was the only team from a major city.

Billy Joe Adcock was not the only player from the 1946 champions to play in college. Harry Moneypenny was the center on that team and he went on to David Lipscomb University in Nashville, Tennessee where he set individual scoring records his first two seasons. Moneypenny was an outstanding baseball player as well and signed a contract with the Boston Red Sox after graduation, but he never made it to the major leagues. He was elected to the Lipscomb athletic Hall of Fame in 1989. The school opened McQuiddey Gymnasium in 1949 with a seating capacity of 3,300. In the opening game visiting Vanderbilt defeated the Lipscomb Bisons 62-39 with former teammates Adcock and Moneypenny on opposing sides. The Commodores could hardly be called a visiting team because they shared the facility with Lipscomb for the next three years while Memorial Gymnasium was completed. McQuiddey was later replaced by the adjoining Allen Arena, a 5,000 seat facility.

A third member of the 1946 team went on to play at the Naval Academy, but he became famous more for his military achievements than his athletic ability. William O. Lawrence was the younger brother of Eddie Lawrence, the star of the 1944 team. He graduated from the Naval Academy in 1951 and became a test pilot in 1952. He is credited with being the first person to fly at twice the speed of sound in a Naval aircraft and was a finalist for the Mercury space program. On June 28, 1967 his F4 Phantom jet was shot down over North Vietnam and he was held as a prisoner of war until 1973.

After his release he continued his military career and served as Superintendent of the Naval Academy from 1978 to 1981. His daughter Wendy attended the Academy during that time as part of the second class to admit females. After graduation she received a Masters from Massachusetts Institute of Technology (MIT) and became a Navy aviator and astronaut. She participated in four space missions and retired from NASA in 2006.

Lawrence was elected to the Tennessee Sports Hall of Fame in 2004. He died on December 2, 2005. During his capture he wrote a poem, "Oh Tennessee, My Tennessee," which was adopted in 1973 as the official state poem of Tennessee. A destroyer was named after him in 2007, the USS William P. Lawrence. Following the West High victory in 1946 Billy Lawrence's career took him miles from his 18th Avenue South home for many years and a national fame far beyond simply being a member of a good basketball team. As a kid growing up a block away at 1710 19th Avenue South I remember looking up to him as a neighborhood kid who was an athletic hero at the school I planned to attend. The

Alumni Room at what is now West End Middle School has a separate exhibit devoted to the late Admiral Lawrence.

In 1947 the tournament moved to the University of Tennessee campus in Knoxville where the school with the funny name, Soddy-Daisy, walloped West in the finals 52-24. The larger seating capacity at UT (4,500) insured the return of the tournament the next year as West returned with a 24-5 record. The postwar economy continued to grow as the United States Senate approved the Marshall Plan to rebuild Europe. Easter ads in the Nashville papers showed a Sears Kenmore washer for $249.50 and an Electrolux vacuum cleaner for $18.50. The rift in the Democratic Party grew wider with Southern Democrats threatening to walk out of the convention over a proposed civil rights plank in the platform. Jackie Robinson had not only played baseball for the Brooklyn Dodgers the year before, but had been named Rookie of the Year. The American League integrated when Larry Doby signed with the Cleveland Indians. It was the beginning of the end for the Negro league as more teams searched for players of color to add to their rosters. High schools and colleges in the South remained totally segregated and showed no indication of a willingness to change. Ironically the National Basketball Association (NBA) which is dominated by African-American players today did not integrate until 1950. In that year Chuck Cooper was the first minority player drafted (Boston Celtics) and Nat "Sweetwater" Clifton left the Harlem Globetrotters and joined the New York Knicks, but Earl Lloyd was actually the first Negro to play in an NBA game after signing with the Rochester Royals.

But, the West High Bluejays were not thinking about anything but basketball when they went to East Tennessee in 1948 for their fifth consecutive trip to the state tournament. The one sided loss in the finals the previous year was still a sore spot with the team and they were tired of hearing that their days of dominance were over. After all they had two championship trophies already which tied them with Knoxville High who won in 1939 and 1941 when East Tennessee teams dominated the competition. However, this was not a particularly tall team and only one player, Bob Dudley Smith, was considered a college prospect.

On Friday the Jays dispatched Memphis Messick 61-51 and the next morning beat Happy Valley 58-54. Certainly this underrated team was showing geography did not matter when it came to scoring points as it moved to the finals against Bristol. Memphis is tucked into the southwest corner of the state next to Mississippi and Arkansas. The only thing between Happy Valley and North Carolina to the east is the Great Smoky Mountains National Park. The town of Bristol (500 miles from Memphis) is in the Northeast corner of Tennessee and the town actually straddles the Virginia border. So in 1948 you would have to say the team from Nashville certainly took on teams from as far away as they could. The other team from Nashville, Father Ryan, took fourth place after losing to Happy Valley 34-30. Father Ryan was coached by Leo Long who moonlighted for years as coach of the Nashville Business College AAU team. One of the players on the 1948 team, Billy Derrick, made the all tournament team and later coached at Ryan for many years. West might have had the Lawrence brothers, but that was nothing compared to Father Ryan High School which had a series of athletic brothers following one another for years. The Derrick, Clunan, Sullivan, Rowan, Gorham, Lynch, Graham, Breen, Wehby, and Mondelli families always seemed to have someone playing a sport and making headlines. The high school back then was located a block from Vanderbilt and many of the families were from the same Hillsboro-West End neighborhood where I grew up. We might have gone to different churches and schools, but we competed for years on the playgrounds in that part of town forming friendships that have lasted a lifetime.

West continued its high scoring ways in the 1948 final game and destroyed Bristol 61-39. Bob Dudley Smith led all scorers with 26 points, almost as many as West High teams had made in victories in earlier years. The game coached by Strickland had evolved over the years into a more offensively oriented concept, largely because of the presence of Smith who was one of the first players in Nashville to be recognized as a "pure shooter." It was popular to criticize players as "shot crazy" when they dominated their team's offense, but Smith did not receive that type of scorn. When he was hot he could simply take over a game. Which he did in the finals as the stunned Vikings could only watch. West played all ten players in the game ending the 29 game winning streak Bristol took into the finals. Another West High player, Floyd Chandler, was also named to the all tournament team. Chandler played well throughout the tournament and was the second high scorer behind Smith with ten points. He was also an outstanding golfer on the West High team. Smith went on to Vanderbilt where he was a solid contributor, but never attained the dominant status he had in high school.

At that time Emmett Strickland had won more state titles than anyone and decided to change careers. He left coaching after the 1948 football season to become principal at Waverly-Belmont Junior High. He later became a school Superintendent in Franklin, Tennessee. Strickland was inducted into the Tennessee Sports Hall of Fame in 1976. His overall record was 151 wins and only 20 losses in the five years his teams won three state championships and finished 2nd (1947) and 3rd (1945) in the other years. He also had a winning record in football (37-25-6) and baseball (14-4). When he left West he was replaced by Charles Greer for the remainder of the 1948-1949 school year. In the fall of 1949 Joe Shapiro began his nineteen year run as the coach of the West End High School Bluejays.

JOE SHAPIRO

      I was in the fifth grade when I first met Coach Shapiro and if he was alive today I would still call him Coach. I don't know anyone of my contemporaries who ever called him Mister when we were teenagers or Joe when we became adults. My father called him Joe because he was the same age and they had known one another for many years before he took the job at Peabody. I realized this when he called the role at our first physical education class and after reading my name he asked me if my father, who had the same name, was a "crippled fellow." By today's standards that would probably classify as an insensitive remark and one I could have complained about, but back then it was simply the way people referred to someone who walked with a limp like Dad did. I don't think you can conclude it was an insensitive remark. My father had polio as a child and the various operations he had left one leg shorter than the other one by about three inches. I always have to stop and think about which leg was the short one because I never thought of him as handicapped or "crippled." I know it was his right one because I can see him driving a golf ball two hundred yards right handed which means your body rotates toward your firm left leg as you make contact and follow through. Dad had a lot of upper body strength although he never weighed more than 145 pounds. He attributed his arm strength to walking on crutches for so much of his life. I learned at an early age that your armpits only contact the top of crutches when you are resting. When you walk you lift yourself off the ground with the help of the crutches and move much faster as a result. He didn't always have to use crutches, but they were kept close by just in case. When he was in his best shape he could walk eighteen holes on a golf course and shoot between 85 and 95. But, there were times when he was not able to get around without using a cane or crutches. His personality didn't change either way and he didn't complain.

So here I am in this gym class and the teacher knows my family which is not that unusual because the fifth grade teacher I have this year once taught my father in the same grade and my brother two years earlier. This is shaping up as a year in which I won't be getting by with anything. This was all right with me because even at that age I did not resist structure if it made sense. Coach Shapiro let us know that first day that his class would be structured and our days of playing on the swings at recess were over. He had reconfigured the locker room and installed shelves that held baskets. We were each assigned a basket number and when we came to class we would go to the opening in the wire enclosure that held the baskets and say our number. Coach Shapiro would then go to the shelf and bring back a basket that held our gym clothes. We would change and return the basket where it would be secure during class. After class we were required to take a shower unless we had a swimming class and the process of getting the basket and changing clothes was repeated. Peabody was an unusual school which actually had an indoor swimming pool as well as a gymnasium so we were required to have the necessary shoes, socks, shorts, t-shirts, and swimsuits for the full range of activities. It was a private school with grades kindergarten through high school in the same three story building. The school's full name was Peabody Demonstration School and it was part of the George Peabody College for Teachers. The school was on one side of Edgehill Avenue and the college was on the other. Across 21st Avenue South was Vanderbilt University. We lived on 19th Avenue South at the far end of the Peabody College campus so I walked to and from school every day through a series of large buildings and open green spaces imagining that I was, or certainly would be someday, a college student like all the ones I saw.

Because of its affiliation with a teachers college there was no shortage of student teachers to assist in our classes which were kept small. The maximum was thirty students, but usually it was between twenty and twenty five. I arrived at Peabody in the third grade and it was my third school in two cities in a little over one year. It was wartime and my father had taken a job in Memphis where I started the first grade at Bruce Elementary School. The job did not work out and we returned to Nashville where I went to Knox School for a half day. That school, which no longer exists, was so crowded that grades 4-6 went in the morning and 1-3 went in the afternoon. That meant my brother and I went at different times because we were three grades apart. We were sharing a large house with my aunt and her family because her husband was in the Navy and there was enough room, but barely, for the four of us. That fall we moved to a small furnished apartment downtown and my father looked for a house to buy. My brother entered the fifth grade at Peabody and I went into the third grade. I should have been in the second, but it was full. My parents convinced the principal that I was smart enough to skip a grade and that's how I ended up in the third grade a year younger than most of my classmates.

Coach Shapiro's gym classes were full of explanations about the rules of basketball and baseball, as well as physical activities in those sports. He brought the same intensity and organization to our classes that he did to the varsity sports he coached. He found space in the basement of the school under the swimming pool and past the boilers that heated the school and the water in the pool to carve out a new locker room for the varsity sports teams. That might sound a little crude, but compared to some of the other small schools on the Peabody schedule it was almost luxurious. Duncan did not have a home field and actually practiced in a dirt parking lot next to the school. The downtown school, Hume –Fogg, practiced a few miles away in Centennial Park. Their players were packed together in the back of a pickup truck for the commute to practice. Peabody not only had a locker room. They had their own field for practice and games. I often stayed after school to watch practice and never missed a home game. High school athletics in Nashville at that time was a confusing patchwork of schools of various sizes. There was a city public school system which had six schools (East, West End, North, Cohn, Howard, and Hume-Fogg). There was a county public system that had more schools, but they varied greatly in size. The larger ones like Isaac Litton, DuPont, and Hillsboro would rarely play the smaller ones like Joelton, Antioch, and Cumberland in football. This meant that a private school that could be competitive like Father Ryan or Montgomery Bell Academy (MBA) would play the big schools from either system in football. Smaller private schools like Peabody and Duncan would play the smaller schools whether they were public or private. However, in basketball there were different districts for the two systems and the city schools (18th District) and the county schools (19th District) rarely met until tournament time. An anomaly to this division was Mt. Juliet, a small school in the county that played in the 18th District tournament. They were rarely a factor except for a few years in the early 1950s when Tom Marshall played for them. Marshall went on to a career at Western Kentucky and the NBA.

Coach Shapiro was from Nashville and his brother was a doctor there. John Shapiro was a pathologist and walked with a limp similar to my father which I think adds to the evidence that Coach Shapiro had no malicious intent when he referred to my father as "crippled." Truthfully, I have to admit that I only remember him saying that one time and if it had not happened the first time I met him I'm not sure I would even remember it. Shapiro had gone to Central High, which sounds like it would be in the city, but it was actually a county school next to the Fair Grounds. He had played football, basketball, and baseball his freshman year at the University of Oklahoma, but a shoulder injury limited him to baseball in subsequent years. He graduated in 1937 and after receiving a Masters Degree at Peabody College he began his coaching career in

Alabama. After two years at Winterboro, Alabama he moved to Talladega. This was in the early 1940s and Talladega was not known for the Speedway that was built later. At that time there was no Speedway in Daytona either and races there were held on the beach. The only auto race anyone talked about in those days was the 500 mile race in Indianapolis on Memorial Day.

Coach Shapiro liked to say that one of his Talladega football teams was the Alabama state champion, but records on that subject are sketchy and inexact. In 1945 and 1946 there was no playoff system, or division into classes, like there is today, but his teams were apparently undefeated both years and certainly had a valid claim to a high ranking. Why he would want to leave a situation like that and return to a small private school in his hometown is something he never talked about. At our 50th class reunion he did acknowledge that the best thing that happened to him in Talladega was meeting his wife. Ruth Tipton was a native of Alabama who left the rural community of Gurley (near Huntsville) to attend college at Berea for two years. She transferred to Alabama Polytechnic Institute (now Auburn University) where she graduated with a degree in Home Economics Education. Her first job right out of college was at Talladega High School. The teacher and the coach were married in August 1946 and moved to Nashville at the end of the school year. It is possible that he viewed the Peabody job as an interim step to a better job in the public school system and he preferred living in Nashville to Alabama. Certainly his predecessor had treated it as a stepping stone. Charles "Bubber" Murphy was a multi sport athlete at Middle Tennessee State Teachers College in Murfreesboro, Tennessee before World War II. After completing his military service he coached at Peabody Demonstration School for one year while he completed his master's degree at Peabody College and then returned to his alma mater and coached for the next twenty years. He is in the school's athletic Hall of Fame and the main activity center is named for him. He was head football coach and athletic director during the period of transition from a teachers college to a full degree granting university. His winning percentage as a coach is the highest in school history. I remember Coach Murphy as a nice man, but his Phys Ed classes were strictly play on the playground and don't get into fights.

It must have been a drastic change for Coach Shapiro to come from a championship team in Alabama to a small private school that had a total squad of barely 25 players. But, his teams were certainly disciplined and innovative, using a combination on offense of the relatively new T-formation and the single wing. Sometimes the Tigers would line up in one formation and then shift into the other in an attempt to draw their opponents offside. After two seasons the vacancy at West End High School opened up and Joe Shapiro was named the new head coach. His teams at Peabody had barely won half their games in football and were below .500 in other sports so it was not a sure thing he would be accepted at his new school which had grown accustomed to the winning ways, at least in basketball, of Emmett Strickland. The timing was good however because within two years Peabody was down to a losing team with fifteen football players and the school dropped the sport. My brother left Peabody for West a year before Coach Shapiro and played on the golf team for four years and the football team for two. In the ninth grade he was also on the junior high basketball team, but never tried to make that team as an upper classman. However, he did keep the scorebook for Coach Shapiro during the 1950-1951 season.

I also stayed at Peabody through the eighth grade and then went to West. I think this was always the plan my family had in mind. But it was made inevitable by my father's illness when I was in the ninth grade. He was diagnosed with osteomylitis in his right hip and because of surgery and recovery would be bedridden for at least six months. Keeping even one child in a private school was out of the question, but the way Peabody was declining athletically, not academically, I knew I didn't want to continue there. Besides I had been following the basketball triumphs of the big school on West End Avenue for several years and had hopes of being part of the tradition.

Certainly Joe Shapiro arrived at West High with a reputation as a football coach that was greater than any other sport. That might have been what some Bluejay supporters had been looking for because their failures in football had been a source of frustration for years. Things did not get better overnight. The Bluejays continued to lose games with the losses to neighboring MBA especially irritating.

The private school was only five blocks away on West End Avenue and drew many students from the same area of the city. While it might have appeared smaller in terms of total enrollment when you subtract females and the junior high from the West student body the male enrollment in grades 10-12 was about the same as MBA. The same could be said about Father Ryan High School also, an all male Catholic school. The MBA Maroons, sometimes called Big Red, were a perennial winner in football and West had never beaten them. When Billy Joe Adcock and Bob Dudley Smith were winning basketball games for West, Bill Wade was doing the same in football for MBA. He went on to Vanderbilt and the Los Angeles Rams and Chicago Bears. Wade was one of the charter members of the Vanderbilt Athletic Hall of Fame. My father enjoyed going to MBA games and at an early age I learned their strange cheer called "aka lacka ching." The full version was "aka lacka ching; aka lacka chow; aka lacka ching ching, chow chow. Boomer lacka, boomer lacka sis boom bah; MBA, MBA, rah, rah, rah." As a small boy I liked hearing that cheer with its silly words. Of course I also liked to go to Vanderbilt games and hear them chant, "Rip 'em up, tear 'em up, give 'em hell, Vandy." But that was because it gave me a chance to say a word I wasn't supposed to use.

The 1949-1950 basketball season opened at home and West was an easy winner over Peabody 44-23. The victory probably had less to do with any knowledge the coach had about his former players than the fact that West was a taller and more experienced team. The Bluejays reeled off four more victories before Christmas defeating Howard 39-35, Lipscomb 40-37, Hume-Fogg 28-18, and East 32-29. The only blemish was a narrow 24-27 loss to Father Ryan. The Bluejays played an exhibition game on December 30, 1949 against an alumni team coached by Emmett Strickland. Apparently the old magic was still there and the veterans won 49-42. Four members of the 1948 state championship team were in the game and Floyd Chandler scored 13 points. Harry Moneypenny from the 1946 team added nine.

The Jays got back on track as the New Year began beating Clarksville on the road by a score of 42-37. The high scorer for Clarksville was Mason Rudolph who would later gain fame on the professional golf tour. The rest of January was a mixture of four wins over North 34-31, Springfield 34-27, Howard 40-38, and Hume-Fogg 35-26. Unfortunately there were three losses that month to Cohn 35-37, MBA 34-53 and Ryan 27-35.

The month of February saw a gradual unraveling of the team that had looked so impressive earlier in the season. There were five losses to Lipscomb 43-47, East 29-32, Springfield 18-24, Ryan 44-48, and MBA 40-41. The three victories came against Cohn 31-28, MBA 46-33, and North 42-36. West was quickly eliminated from the District tournament by Hume-Fogg, a team they had already beaten twice. The Bluejays had a one point lead at the end of the first quarter and never led thereafter. The final score was 43-28.

Shapiro's 1950 football team was a disappointing 3-7 affair although more had been expected with thirteen seniors on the 30 man squad. The death of end Kenneth Eller in an Air National Guard plane crash in July was a setback to the team, but that was hardly the reason for the loss of the first three games. The porous West High defense was simply outscored by Cohn 15-25, MBA 7-27, and Springfield 6-40. After a mid season win over North 26-6 the Jays proceeded to lose four of the remaining six games. The defense held on to squeak by Hillsboro 20-19 and Ryan 6-0, but the other losses were a repeat of the start of the season. East walloped them14-39. Clarksville beat them 20-28. It was Central by a score of 14-20 and the season ended with a 13-19 loss to Gallatin. Center and Captain Kim Smith made the All-City team in the lone bright spot at the end of the season.

The basketball team was not expected to be much better than the previous year. An opening win over Howard 39-35 was followed by a loss to David Lipscomb 27-42. A victory over Springfield 37-30 was followed by losses to Ryan 30-51, and East 23-44. The 2-3 record had the Jays looking forward to the New Year. At least this year they would not have to face the alumni squad.

January was a better month and started with an easy victory over North 50-31. The next game was an astounding 52-12 win over Duncan, a small private school soon to be closed and the school property sold to Vanderbilt University for the new gymnasium. An easy victory over MBA 46-27 was followed by losses to Cohn 36-40, Howard 33-39, and Lipscomb 31-33. A narrow 28-26 win over Ryan gave the Jays a .500 record going into the month of February.

It started well with an easy win over Cohn 52-20 followed by a narrow victory at MBA 23-21. The Bluejays traveled to Springfield and pulled out a 34-33 win and then lost at home to North 31-33. The low scoring slowdown continued, but this time East came out on top 20-25. The Jays upped the tempo and beat Springfield for the third time 53-44 and traveled to Clarksville for a 47-37 road victory. Mason Rudolph easily led all scorers in the game with 18 points.

The regular season was a winning one, but not overly impressive with twelve wins and eight losses. An overtime loss to David Lipscomb in the district tournament meant that West would fail to advance to the Regional tournament for the third straight year.

Given the lackluster record of Coach Shapiro in his first two years at West no one was looking for a lot of improvement when he began the next football season at the school. Opening with an upset win over East High, 19-6 the Bluejays ended with a 7-3 record, a reversal of the previous year. The victory over East was followed by a 25-6 win against Cohn and disappointing losses to MBA 7-13 and Springfield 0-25. Thereafter the defense improved and West won five of the last six games. They shut out North 25-0. Columbia fell by a score of 34-8 at homecoming. After a close loss to Jackson, 7-13, the Jays won the final three games. The only close one was Clarksville 15-14. Easy wins over Ryan 39-12 and Central 20-0 put West in the Thanksgiving Day Clinic Bowl game.

Unfortunately it was a rematch against East High and the one sided game went the other way this time. East scored on a fumble recovery on the first play of the game and never looked back cruising to a 7-39 victory. There was no playoff system in Tennessee at that time, but the Clinic Bowl which was held at Vanderbilt Stadium determined who the best team was in Nashville. It was sponsored by the Nashville Junior Chamber of Commerce and was initially the brainchild of my father's law partner, Benson Trimble. It was named the Clinic Bowl because it was a fund raiser for Vanderbilt Hospital and modeled after a college all star game that was held in San Francisco at that time. The slogan of that game "strong legs run so weak legs can walk" was adopted at the inception. Today there are similar games all across the country and the Shrine All Star game continues. The 84th game was played in

Houston, Texas on January 17, 2009. Eventually the local game expanded beyond Nashville teams and became incorporated into the state playoff system to determine a true state champion.

When basketball season came around no one expected West to improve very much on their erratic season in 1950-1951. They were better than my junior high team that same year that only won one game, if in fact we actually did win that one. The 1951-1952 team was a combination of football players and new comers which included two from the excellent Cavert Junior High team of the previous year, Jimmy French and Kenneth Zink. The combination of French and Zink was a visual delight to many since there was a difference of almost ten inches in height between the two.

French made his debut scoring nine points in a road loss to Howard 24-29.He was scoreless in the next game against Lipscomb, but West won 36-32 with Joel Berlin scoring 13 points. All City performer Russ Wingo led the losers with 20. Coach Shapiro got a chance to play all eleven players in the next game, a one sided 51-19 victory over Springfield. The winning streak was snapped by Ryan 31-36 followed by losses to East 23-44 and Hillsboro 39-41.

When the new year started West still had not settled on a starting lineup and continued to play as many as nine different players in most games. The way they played in January was also erratic and unpredictable. A loss to North 34-36 was followed by a win against MBA 55-29. A trip to Clarksville produced another loss 51-55 as their old nemesis Mason Rudolph scored 18. They beat Cohn 57-35 and turned around to lose to Howard 47-48. The alternating pattern of wins and losses continued for another two weeks with West defeating Lipscomb 51-40, Clarksville 50-48 (Rudolph had 14), and Cohn 44-31. The losses were Ryan 40-50 and East 36-39.

Now it was February and the coach was still playing various combinations of his eleven players. Kenneth Zink was a member of the "B" team so he could get more playing time, but Jimmy French continued to play with the varsity. A one sided win over MBA 48-30 was followed by an improbable 42-44 loss to Springfield; a team the Blue Jays had destroyed 51-19 earlier in the season. A close game with North resulted in a 47-45 win and then the most astounding game in an already confounding season occurred when Duncan beat the Blue Jays 52-53 in overtime on the Jays home court. Duncan only played five people and four of them had been on the team the previous year when they lost by 33 points. It was a fitting farewell for the school without a gym that would soon be without a building as ground preparation for the new Vanderbilt Memorial Gymnasium began.

The frustrating loss to Duncan probably contributed to the 66-34 win over TIS to end the season, but not much was expected when the District tournament started. West had a 10-11 record for the season so they were not a seeded team when the tournament started at David Lipscomb College. By this time French had become a starter proving his height, or lack of it, was not going to stop him on the basketball court. In the opening game he led all scorers with 16 points as West beat Mt. Juliet 59-22. Despite two regular season losses to East the Bluejays won a close contest 40-39. Next in sight was Hume-Fogg, the downtown school which had knocked West out of the tournament the previous year.

This time it wasn't close as West led all the way to a 51-37 win. French had twelve points. He only had two the following night when West beat North 45-33 to claim their first 18th District tournament trophy since 1948. French made the all tournament team that year as West moved on to the regional. That tournament would also be on the neutral floor at Lipscomb where Vanderbilt was playing their home games until the new on campus gym was completed.

At that time both the runner-up and the champion in the district tournament went to the regional tournament. In the opening game West had to play DuPont who was the 19th District runner-up to Hillsboro. The multiple use of players earlier in the year had given way to five starters who played almost the entire game. West led 14-13 at the end of the first quarter and 24-22 at the half. It was all tied at 33 apiece when the final quarter opened. In the second half DuPont switched from a zone defense to a man-to-man and that shut down the outside shooting that had kept West in the game. Late in the game Joel Berlin picked up his fifth foul and DuPont won 40-44.

However, the future looked bright for the next year with eight players returning. Additionally West had an undefeated B team that year in part because the lanky Zink had ended up on that squad where he could play regularly instead of riding the bench with the varsity. With a football team in a bowl game and a basketball team with a tournament trophy it was beginning to look like Joe Shapiro might make people forget about the records of Emmett Strickland.

My brother closed out his athletic career at West that spring playing on the golf team for the fourth year. I joined him for the beginning of my three year run on the same team. His football career had actually been set back by golf his senior year because he qualified to play in the National Junior golf tournament and missed the first week of football practice. He spent the year as a backup quarterback and decided to see if he could play in college when he got to Harvard the next fall. He did make the team, but after a broken leg decided to just play golf for the Crimson after that. I never saw my mother so happy to see someone break a leg.

1952-1953

The high hopes for West End High in the new school year were dashed early in the first game when the Bluejays lost to East before a standing room only crowd at the West high stadium. The final score of 17-33 was followed by equally one sided losses to Cohn (13-28) and Springfield (6-27). Sandwiched in between those losses was a surprising scoreless tie with MBA. A one sided victory over North (45-0) was followed by a shutout loss to Columbia (0-24. There were two more losses, Clarksville (7-13) and Ryan (13-27). The two victories over Hillsboro (18-14) and Central (19-7) wrapped up a disappointing 3-6-1 season. Adding to the bad news was the broken leg suffered by quarterback Ralph Greenbaum who had transferred from Howard High School and was expected to be a major contributor to the basketball team. I first saw Ralph when he was playing on the Howard Junior High team my freshman year. The next year he transferred to West, but had to sit out a year before he was eligible to play sports. His sophomore year he was the scorekeeper as West won the District Tournament and advanced to the Regional where they lost to DuPont.

The rumors of dissension on the football team unfortunately spilled over to the basketball team and complaints about the harsh discipline of Coach Shapiro spread throughout the school. It is certainly true that he could be abrupt in many of his dealings with people of any age. By my junior year in high school I had been in a position to observe him for almost seven years and I just thought of him as firm, but consistent. I knew him not only as a teacher and coach, but as an employer. In the summer he had a job as caddy master at McCabe Field golf course and I would work there occasionally. It was hard work carrying a heavy bag for eighteen holes and there were days when you sat around for several hours before you got a chance to work. The caddies kept a dice game out of sight of the keen eyes of Joe Shapiro and the golf pro Luther Hickman. I did not go near the game, in part because I wanted to stay in the good graces of Shapiro and Hickman, but more because I knew those sharp characters from West Nashville would take me to

48

the cleaners if I got in the game. McCabe was on the dividing line between what people called West End and West Nashville. There actually was a railroad track that ran to Memphis beside the golf course that was both a physical and financial barrier. People on the north side went to Cohn and many families there worked in the factories in that part of town. At West there might have been some sons and daughters of factory workers, but I never knew about it. The teenagers I met that summer were a pretty rough bunch compared to what I was used to, but several of them were also good golfers and we competed against each other for the next few years.

The basketball season started with a lineup that was much more settled than the previous year. The guards would be returning lettermen Jimmy French and Frank Willard. Letterman John Wright joined B teamer Billy Owens at forward and Kenneth Zink was the center. However, an opening loss to Hillsboro 25-57 allowed all eleven team members to see action. A week later the whole team played again, but this time West beat Howard 55-44. For the remainder of December the Jays played at a .500 pace beating Lipscomb 43-42, Springfield 35-31, and TIS 70-37. Losses came at the hands of Ryan 39-46, East 53-58, and North 47-52.

When January came it looked like the defending District champions had worked out their problems with victories over MBA 54-51 and Clarksville 58-47 (no Rudolph on the team). The optimism was not justified as West lost five of the next six games. Cohn beat them 42-50. Howard won easily 45-65. Lipscomb avenged an earlier loss 42-52, and Ryan won in overtime 35-37. After a win over Peabody 54-31, the Jays were destroyed by East 52-68. In an earlier game the center for East, Bill Rutherford, scored 24 points, but he was injured early in the second game which ended his basketball career. I had known Bill for years because his aunt was my father's legal secretary. He also was a caddy at Shelby golf course and an above average golfer. After he went to Belmont College we went to law school at the same time and the friendship continued until I left Nashville in 1969. By then Bill was a Circuit Court Judge, but I still remember how badly I felt when I saw him go down with a knee injury on my birthday in 1953. I'm sure my concern came as a shock to some of my classmates, but they had no way of knowing the full story. The Stokes/Rutherford connection did not begin or end with me and Bill. There has been a Stokes practicing law in Nashville since 1838. The Rutherford string started in 1890.

The erratic pattern of wins followed by losses continued in February. West beat Cohn 62-51 and MBA 64-54. Then they went to Springfield and lost 29-35 and returned home to lose to North 50-54. B teamer Buddy Parsons had moved up to a starting role adding some offensive punch, but Blue Jay fans were already thinking about next year when Ralph Greenbaum would be joining veteran players like French, Owens, Zink, and Parsons. One sided wins against TIS 60-44 and Peabody 79-42 closed out the season, but the 11-11 record made the defending champs an unseeded team. They opened with an easy 50-28 victory over Peabody in the tournament which had moved from Lipscomb to the newly opened Vanderbilt Memorial Gymnasium. The following night they lost to Howard 46-55 and a disappointing season came to an end. They had only been able to string together three consecutive wins twice during the season and most of those victories came against weak teams. Two were against TIS and three against Peabody. Dropping football had not helped the Tigers on the basketball court, but their team was loaded with sophomores and freshmen, including my cousin McNeill. Vanderbilt standout Dan Finch had graduated and began to coach the team while he was in law school and the eventual turnaround was amazing. The turnaround for West was more like a downturn. Adding to the turmoil surrounding Coach Shapiro during the season was his absence for several games because of a back injury. Assistant Coach Charles Cummings filled in for two games, MBA and Cohn, and won both games. Now it was time for spring football practice followed by the start of baseball and golf season.

When spring football practice started it was obvious that the disappointing seasons that year in football and basketball had been a learning experience for the students who were looking to the future. There was a renewed sense of purpose and dissidents were clearly not welcome anymore. Coach Shapiro also appeared to have decided he would no longer worry about criticism that he played favorites. He wanted teams made up of boys who would listen to him when he talked and not spread gossip behind his back. Many of these players had been together since grammar school and most of them came from Cavert Junior High, but there were others who bought into the idea of winning as a team who came from the other feeder schools. Probably the most important characteristic was that the team members accepted the team captains, Oakley Christian in football and Jimmy French in basketball, without grumbling. This new spirit of cooperation carried over from a spirited spring football practice to a surprisingly good baseball team. I got to see the football part up close because I had become the manager of the team. In baseball the person called manager runs the show and is aided by people called coaches. In football and basketball the coach runs the show and people called managers pick up wet towels after practice.

Maybe it was my association with Coach Shapiro that began in elementary school, but for whatever reason he entrusted me with a great deal of responsibility, both during spring practice and the season that followed. I even had my own key to the locker room and the outside door to the school which I have to believe was unusual for a student, and probably against Board of Education policy. I not only got to pick up wet towels, I got to wash them, fold them, and hand them out. I repaired equipment and replaced it when it was broken or the wrong size. Because the coach insisted on taping ankles for all the players for games, and several for practice, I learned how to tear adhesive tape in ten inch strips with my bare hands. Taking all the equipment to the practice field and returning it was an obvious part of the job, and there were two scrimmages with other schools during that spring practice. Coach treated those as dress rehearsals for a game situation and the list of duties expanded greatly. In keeping with the Shapiro style of organization game day and practice duties were spelled out in writing. In some ways it felt like I was back at Peabody and checking out my basket of clothes from this quiet man we all called coach. If you did what you were supposed to do he might nod in approval. If you made a mistake more than once you were in for more than the mild admonition you received for the first miscue. It is interesting that today players often make a bad pass or drop a ball and immediately acknowledge that failure. The worst thing you could do with Joe Shapiro was to drop a ball and say "I'm sorry." You would immediately be met with a loud voice that said "don't be sorry. Everyone knows you're sorry. Be right." We didn't laugh behind his back when he said that, but I have to admit there were a lot of smiles after practice when he had commented on inept play as looking like "grab ass in the asparagus patch." I am not sure where that one came from. We were city boys and the only place we ever saw asparagus was on a plate. Shapiro wasn't unique in his utterances. Coach Jack Story who led the Cuba, Kentucky Cubs to the finals of the state tournament twice was known for saying "I don't want you to try. I want you to do it." His players probably knew something about asparagus patches also.

When football spring practice was over I resumed my spring routine of playing golf every afternoon unless we had a match. I would deviate from that routine on days the baseball team played in front of the school. The bad taste from poor football and basketball teams was soon gone as the Nashville Interscholastic League (NIL) champions rolled through the season and into the tournament. Coach Shapiro had shown his zero tolerance attitude with that team when he kicked one of the better players off the team after a series of altercations. Despite his obvious talent no one mourned the loss other than to acknowledge that it was probably one of the greatest wastes of potential talent we ever saw. Greenbaum had recovered from his broken leg to play in the outfield and the addition of Jimmy Lewis to the pitching staff propelled the team to the final game of the state tournament.

In the final game of the year defeat was literally snatched from "the jaws of victory" when the West High catcher tried to pick a runner off third base and made a wild throw. It was a sad sudden ending to a successful season. But, school was already out and I didn't have time to commiserate with my friends about it because I had to leave the following day for my summer job in Lake Wales, Florida.

FOOTBALL 1953

     The summer in Florida was an interesting experience and the longest period I had ever been away from home. I had gone away to a summer camp three times for two months, but that was a totally supervised environment. When I left for a summer job in June of 1953 all I knew was I would be sharing a house with five other people, three of whom I hardly knew at the time. My idea of Florida was a place with sunny skies and sandy beaches. What I got was Lake Wales in the middle of the state with daily thunderstorms and a lot of orange groves. I was employed as an actor-technician in an outdoor drama about the Seminole Indians entitled "Florida Aflame." The technician part meant I had to work a few hours at the theatre during the day preparing the large stage, which was all sand, except for a small wooden platform in the middle of the set. The heat and humidity was brutal even for a kid from middle Tennessee and after we did our work we got to kill time and bet on whether that night's performance would be rained out. In Florida it rarely rains at night, but in the summer (which runs from March to October) there will be a thunderstorm just about every afternoon. This often undid much of our work on the stage which had to be redone in time for a performance that almost no one attended anyway. If there was a performance I would change into my costume as a Spanish soldier. This was a really good deal because if I had been cast as an Indian I would have had to wear full body makeup. I also got to wrestle Chief Osceola as he attempted to escape from prison in the next to last scene. Fortunately he killed me so I got to exit the stage in the blackout and not appear in the final scene which was actually the Chief's funeral. After he killed me another soldier killed him. The first week I got out of my costume and was ready to go before anyone else until the director saw what I was doing and made me stay in costume for the final curtain call.

I already had some theatre experience prior to that summer and I learned a lot while working with professionals who actually made a living in the theatre. The only person who was famous at the time was a dancer named Barton Mumaw, but later Godfrey Quigley (Clockwork Orange) won awards for acting and Robert Drumheller was nominated for an Oscar for set design. Quigley played Osceola and Drumheller was the lighting designer for the play. There were others who had varying degrees of success in the fields of acting and dancing, but I knew I wasn't going to do that for a living and didn't stay in touch. Besides they were all older than me and regarded me with suspicion. There was some question whether or not I deserved to be there because my father was the person who promoted the idea in the first place and was president of the corporation that produced the show. It was a financial disaster, he lost money, and I never got paid for anything I did. When time came in August to leave Lake Wales and get back to football practice I was more than ready to leave. I had been sharing a house with one bathroom with five others in the show, two males and three females. They were never able to get all of the body makeup out of the tub and the sink. I did get to see the ocean three times that summer on our one day a week off (Monday) and it was more than I ever imagined it would be. I must have looked like a sixteen year old hillbilly from Tennessee that June day in Daytona Beach, Florida when I saw the Atlantic for the first time. I was rendered totally speechless at the enormity of the scene in front of me. The closest I've come to a repeat of that experience was years later when I saw the Grand Canyon for the first time.

When I got back to Nashville there were several surprises waiting for me when the football team started practicing twice a day. A leg injury to Eddie Gaines was not healing fast enough for him to play football, but if he sat out the season he would probably be in good shape to play basketball. He didn't give up football completely and agreed to be an assistant manager for the team. Cliff Keel was left with no backup at center except sophomore Philip Suter. The situation was worse at tackle. Both of the starters, Ray Spence and John Doak, had transferred to schools outside of Nashville. Butch Stephens was moved from end to tackle and Oakley Christian went from guard to the other tackle spot. Luther Jones stayed at guard and the other spot on the line was taken by senior Gailor Justice who was playing football for the first time that year. Billy Owens and Buddy Parsons were returning lettermen at end and there was no experienced back up for them. But, there wasn't any backup at tackle or guard either. Sophomores Jerry Duke at end and Don Corn at tackle were going to have to play a lot sooner than Coach Shapiro had planned in the spring. The reserves at guard were two seniors who like Justice had never earned a letter, Walter Grove and David Compton. A further complication was caused by the arrival of a new assistant coach, Jim Kennedy, assigned to work with the linemen. Kennedy had never coached at West before and was not assigned to the school for spring practice. Everything he was going to learn about this team was going to start when fall practice started.

Edgar Allen wrote an article in the Nashville Banner before the season which quoted Shapiro as saying, "We're so thin in reserves, it scares me. We'll have a fair first team, but after that, I don't know." The team the previous year had a losing record of 3-6-1 and 19 of 26 lettermen from that team were gone. Of the seven who were returning only Greenbaum at quarterback had been a starter. The average weight of the offensive line was 174 pounds and the backfield was 157. The entire team average was only 168 pounds.

The backfield was not just small. There was no breakaway speed or deep passing threat there either. After a week of practice Coach Shapiro called a lengthy classroom session to put in the multiple formation offense he had employed at Peabody. With only a week to go before the home opener with Cohn on September 11[th,] a date of no particular distinction at that time, the starting lineup was still uncertain and the team was struggling with the new offense. It showed when that game ended in a scoreless tie. Before the game

Coach Shapiro was making his remarks to the team and I remember him saying that because Cohn wore all white uniforms this made them look bigger than they actually were. I took some equipment out to the bench before the team did so I was by myself when a bus pulled up and the visiting team ran across the field to their bench. I had to laugh because it wasn't just the uniforms. This team was big, I mean really big.

Neither team got any offense going although West did score a touchdown that was called back because of a penalty. A missed field goal try in the closing seconds by Ralph Greenbaum made the upcoming game with MBA look a little menacing to say the least. The West High kicking game was far from settled before the opener and no one was actually trained to kick field goals of any length at that time. The Greenbaum try was a drop kick which he had often done in practice, but never in a game. I'm not sure anyone has done it in a game, high school, college, or pro since before the Second World War other than that unfortunate attempt. In a drop kick there is no holder and the kicker simply drops the ball to the ground where it bounces up slightly and gets kicked end over end. In many ways it resembles the traditional extra point try with a holder as far as the end result and it does give you an additional blocker. Soccer style kickers were unheard of at that time, but when that kicking style became popular the straight ahead kickers went the way of the dropkick. Needless to say this was not tried again that season by West and efforts were made to find an extra point kicker with the range to kick field goals if we got in that position again. I even thought about doing it and would practice kicking off a tee before practice started, but I really did not have a strong leg. Kicking extra point distance was about all I could manage.

In an effort to improve the offense Coach Shapiro had coaxed Jimmy French into joining the team even though an injury to him might have been damaging to the basketball team. But there were already six or seven basketball players on the football team anyway, so that wasn't that big a concern. That explains why Frenchie's picture is inserted like a ghost hovering over my shoulder in the team picture. West had only used four substitutes in the Cohn game so Coach Shapiro was scrambling for players he could use wherever he might find them. The opening game had been on a

Thursday night so Hillsboro High School could play a Friday home game at the West High field. Their school had been damaged by a fire and the Burros were temporarily holding classes at Belmont College (now Belmont University). Also Father Ryan often played their home games at West because they did not have a stadium at all. To save the turf on the field Coach Shapiro usually held practices in other parts of the school grounds. If he did go on the field it was usually in the end zones.

The next game was on a Saturday night, September 20th, and when we boarded a bus for the short ride to MBA no one gave West a chance in the game. This was a team they had never beaten, although they had tied them the year before. Before the game several team members made emotional speeches about the importance of winning this year. Then they proceeded to go out and play a listless and scoreless first half, trailing by thirteen points. There was no visiting locker room at MBA so the halftime break was spent in a classroom in the main school building. Coach Shapiro commented sarcastically about the irrelevance and inaccuracy of the pre game speeches. It was irritating to hear, but it apparently had an effect. West scored three times after intermission and won 20-13. It was the biggest victory a Shapiro coached Bluejay football team had ever had. In fact it was probably the biggest win he had experienced since leaving Talladega, Alabama almost a decade before.

The following week Edgar Allen had to admit in his column that he had been way off base when he predicted an easy victory for MBA in the game. However, Coach Shapiro was quoted as saying, "I still contend we don't have a good football team, but simply a gritty bunch of boys that have a lot of desire to win and want to play football."

The following week the Bluejays squeaked by a visiting Springfield team 20-19 which marked the first victory over that school since 1944. The game was played on Thursday night, September 25th, but I think Coach Shapiro liked playing the first game on a weekend when the field might be used three straight nights. The low spot of the game came when Johnny Pyburn suffered a broken jaw making the already thin backfield even thinner. But, with an undefeated season (one tie) after three games the Blue Jays were way ahead of pre season expectations. Spirits were high going into the game against North. In the three previous seasons West had beaten the Yankees, 45-0, 25-0, and 26-6. Our optimism was not rewarded as North shut out West 0-13 on what was one of the most difficult nights of my young life. Another backfield member was injured when Tommy Coke had a shoulder separation and was taken to a hospital at halftime. Even with the injuries West only used 17 players for the night. It was a busy night on the sidelines for a manager, but my troubles started a long time before the game began.

We kept two bags of ice on the sidelines at every game and it was my job as manager to go purchase them at a convenience store not far from the school. I usually did this after Coach Shapiro gave me the money about an hour and a half before kickoff for a home game. For an away game I would go to the store shortly before the bus left. This night we must have taken longer taping ankles or maybe there was some other reason why the time got away from us, but it was almost time for the bus to leave with the team and I still had not purchased the ice. Coach gave me some money and the managers went in a car to the store taking a bag of footballs and some other equipment with us. He told us to wait at the store and then follow the bus when it went by on West End Avenue. I got the ice and the car circled around a railroad trestle behind the store where we waited for the bus. After about ten minutes it was obvious the bus had either left quicker than I anticipated or it was going to be late getting to the game. I knew the way to the school anyway and we took off wondering where the team was. The carload of managers arrived at the conclusion we needed a reason why we were late arrivals at the stadium. Getting lost was rejected because we were supposed to be following the bus anyway. A flat tire seemed to be the best explanation for our delay. We got to the school and instead of going into the stadium like we would have been able to do if we were in fact following the bus, one of the other managers and I jumped out of the car with our equipment and headed to the ticket booth which was the only way to get in. Eddie went to park the car and joined us later.

It wasn't hard talking our way in because we were wearing coveralls that said West manager and carrying equipment that one would have on the bench for a game. My heart sank when I saw a city bus parked next to the school and our team already on the field trying to warm up without any footballs to toss around. No one was pleased to see me and I mumbled something to Coach Shapiro about a flat tire, but he didn't say anything. The game was never close, although Gailor Justice did make the all city team that week for his defensive efforts. One has to wonder who they were talking about when the reporter covering the game described Justice as "chunky." The six footer weighed 160 pounds making the senior guard the lightest player in the starting line. When I got back to the school the locker room was silent. It stayed that way until everyone had left and I had finished all my chores as manager. Then I went to the coach I had known for years. It was just the two of us in that steamy locker room that smelled of sweaty clothes. It's not a pleasant smell when you lose, but when you win you don't even notice it. I told him there was no flat tire. We had just missed the bus when it went by. All he said was "we'll talk about it on Monday."

A difficult night now turned into a long unhappy weekend while I wondered if I would still be the team manager when I got back to school on Monday. That semester I had arranged my schedule so I took Driver Training the last period of the day. That was a joke because I already had a driver's license. It was just a way for me to report to the locker room an hour before school was out and get ready for practice. The locker room we used was not the cramped one next to the gym that I described when I played junior high basketball. Shapiro had done something similar to his Peabody experience and moved into space in the basement that was vacant after the school dropped ROTC my junior year. It had a shower room with no more than six showers which meant taking one quick when there were thirty sweaty players vying for space. The individual lockers were really open stalls where you could hang up your clothes with benches in front. There was a separate room which had the always busy washing machine and dryer that held the uniforms and other equipment for three sports. The manager had his own area which could be locked up when valuables were left in my custody. Finally there was a training room for treatment of injuries and the ankle taping ritual before each game. All in all, it was a pretty good setup for a small high school. I had access to all of it and

I loved the responsibility. If I was going to lose my job it was going to be painful.

The door to the locker room area was locked most of the time except when school was in session. I think it probably had a door and a lock because when it was used for ROTC rifles and other military equipment was stored there. The outside double doors opened into the back yard of the school leading straight to the football field. You could go to school there for years and if you were not an athlete you would never set foot in the place. Maybe you wouldn't even know what was there.

I certainly didn't know what was waiting for me that Monday afternoon, but Coach Shapiro never said a word about the incident and we prepared for our next opponent, cross town rival East High. This would be another bus trip and this time the ice and everything else was on board in plenty of time for the trip. I think we had all learned our lesson from the North fiasco.

East High had a football stadium that was not as strange as their gym, but it had its challenges. The stands were only on one side of the field behind the school. The bus parked on the side of the field with no grandstands, but there were plenty of hecklers to cuss at us when we pulled in. It was a strange game and we won 8-0. This was long before the two point conversion rule so we actually had a safety for two points and a missed extra point after a touchdown. The kicking woes that had started with the Cohn game continued to be a problem as Coach Shapiro searched for a reliable kicker. Don Corn not only got credit for the safety, but made all city that week as well. When we left East High the bus had to slowly make its way through an even larger throng of hecklers. I was happy to get out of that place and have another victory. I liked to think we didn't behave like that when teams played at West, but I really didn't know because I had never observed a team leaving our stadium.

Shapiro continued to tinker with his offense and tried to put in a "silent" snap count. The quarterback would call a play in the huddle and then yell "set" at the line of scrimmage. If the snap count was three the center would hand the ball to the quarterback, or center it to the tailback, three beats later. But, the rhythmic beats would be inaudible and we worked for many minutes in practice trying to get everyone to count silently to the magic number and then go. The only problem was one lineman, Gailor Justice, could not keep from bobbing his tail up and down as he counted to himself. He would stop doing it in practice if you yelled at him, but it was too risky to try the "silent" count in a game.

After two weeks on the road it was nice to be home for a change when we played Hillsboro. At that time we had a winning record (3-1-1) which was a wonder because we had outscored our opponents by only three points (48-45) in the first five games. The offense came alive that night scoring four times in the first half, every time we had the ball, cruising to a 32-13 win, notwithstanding three missed extra points.

The tables were turned the next week when we went to Clarksville and got walloped 0-27. It could have been worse because Clarksville had a touchdown called back. Another time an open receiver dropped a pass in the end zone. It was the only road trip of the year outside of Nashville and the only one where we actually dressed and showered in a strange locker room. The forty mile bus ride back was pretty quiet until we stopped for a meal at a diner that was expecting a bus load of hungry players. It got a lot noisier as the stomachs got full and the pain of the second loss began to subside.

With two games left on the schedule it would be necessary to win at least one game to have a winning season. That was assured when we squeaked by Father Ryan 6-0 (don't even ask about the extra point). Ryan had an outstanding running back named Manson Rowan. On one play their guard pulled and Gailor Justice shot through the opening and tackled Rowan for a loss behind the line of scrimmage. As he got up he said "run that one again Rowan" loud enough for Banner sportswriter Edgar Allen to hear it. Edgar covered games from the sidelines and I knew him because he also covered golf for the paper. He turned to me and asked who made the tackle. I told him and spelled the unusual first name for him. Gailor made the All-City team that week and later for the year. I had to wonder if that one tackle (and trash talk) had anything to do with it. He was a consistent player all season on a team that had no particular stars so he probably deserved it as much as anyone else. But, the All-City team in those days was very much a subjective decision by the writers for the papers who covered the games with input from the coaches. Detailed statistics about tackles,

61

interceptions, etc., were not kept, and probably not even thought of. Today records are kept about everything, including 40 yard dash times and bench press numbers. Games are taped and many schools have the money and staff to videotape practices. Today it certainly takes more than one tackle and a taunting remark to make an all star team, but in 1953 who knows?

The 5-2-1 record going into the last game was still something of an oddity because by that time we were only outscoring our opponents by one point (86-85). It might have been a little better if we had a reliable kicker. The final game was a local road one again against Central, a team we had beaten the previous two years. Coach Shapiro reminded the team that week that we had beaten North the past three years and that did not keep us from losing in a game that now seemed to be months ago. The passage of time in a football season appears longer than other sports in my opinion because of the change in the weather from start to finish. You start practicing in August when heat stroke is a worry and you end up in November just trying to keep your hands warm. By contrast in basketball you tend to play indoors in nothing but cold weather and in baseball you rarely start until the weather gets warm and stays that way. Of course in today's professional sports this calendar has been rendered obsolete with longer and longer seasons. Another part of the intensity of a football season is the smaller number of games and the time between them. The wins and losses take on greater significance than in other sports. Our football team had two losses and a tie. Later that year the basketball team had more losses (three). But, if you asked someone which team was more successful they would certainly say basketball.

On a brisk November afternoon in 1953 I went out to the practice field with a bag of footballs and a chilling thought went across my brain when I realized that this might well be the last week of my life when I would be on a football practice field as part of some team. Going back to the days at Peabody when I just watched the practices and chased down balls for the kickers and continuing through watching my brother's team and now this one it seemed like this was where I spent my fall afternoons. It was a sad feeling although I was looking forward to going to college, having a career, raising a family, etc. But that all seemed to be in the far distant future even though it was just around the corner. As the commercial says "life comes at you fast."

My nostalgic mood was broken later by a humorous incident that occurred at the final practice. Our center Cliff Keel had played for four years without a serious injury, but he had lost four of his front teeth in an automobile accident. The redhead could be a menacing figure when he opened his mouth on a football field. Face masks were rarely worn in those days or any other kind of protection for your teeth. At practice that day Keel had another tooth knocked out and he was actually happy about it. He could now claim to have lost a tooth playing football instead of having to explain that the gap in his smile was from a car accident.

Keel's toothlessness during a game sometimes made him hard to understand. The previous year Coach Shapiro had sent him in with instructions to run a certain play. The breathless center got to the huddle and told quarterback Greenbaum something that sounded like "fuddy-fup on fup." Running plays were simply a series of numbers with the first number designating the back to get the ball; the second number would be the opening in the line where he would run; and three would be the snap count. Asking him to repeat it didn't make it any clearer and a laughing Greenbaum called time out and walked to the sidelines to talk to his confused coach. Cliff's nickname thereafter was "fuddy-fup," sometimes just shortened to "fup." I had known Cliff since my days as a caddy at McCabe Field. He caddied for my brother when he played in the finals of the NIL tournament in 1951. Cliff never made the golf team as a player, but he was an excellent caddy.

The game at Central got off to a slow start with a scoreless first half. West pulled away in the second half and was leading 20-6 with little time left on the clock. When they lined up for the extra point in an unusual formation Coach Shapiro started yelling. But, back then a coach couldn't call timeout from the sidelines like today and all he could do was watch. Again the center of attention was "fuddy-fup" who had been kicking extra points in practice for four years, but had never been considered as someone to do it in a game. There he was grinning from ear to ear awaiting the snap from the center who was Oakley Christian now that Keel had moved from his usual position. Tony Gothard who would normally have been the kicker took Oakley's place as an offensive lineman for the first (and only) time in his life. Then the fun started.

Christian wore thick glasses and his helmet had a clear plastic protector for his eyes. Unfortunately the plastic did a better job of trapping steam than anything else. When he perspired the glasses or the protector would steam up and at the first time out he usually gave the glasses to me and they stayed in my coverall pocket the rest of the game. Unfortunately this meant he couldn't read the scoreboard and was always asking his teammates how much time was on the clock. At the start of his career he had been a center, but this time when he bent over the ball he couldn't really see who he was centering it to. So he fired a bullet that deflected off the holder's hands into a startled Keel. Billy Owens at right end made a block, fell into the end zone, and looked up to see if the point was good. Since there was no ball in the air he looked back and saw a confused Keel running toward him with the ball. Keel heaved a two handed end over end pass which Owens caught on his knees. It was the ugliest and funniest play I have ever seen on a football field. This was before the two point conversion rule, but it counted as one point making the final score 21-6. Both Keel and Owens made the all city team that week, which makes the selection appear to have been made by someone with a sense of humor.

The winning season that started with an unsuccessful as well as unusual drop kick field goal try ended with an even stranger, but successful, extra point try. The school which started practice in the fall with seven returning lettermen had made it through nine games, surviving injuries to key players, to the point where 28 players saw action in the final game. The bus ride back to school was a happy ride. Even the Coach was laughing and smiling. The start of basketball practice was three days away.

BASKETBALL 1953-1954

Somewhere in my elementary school years I formed a desire to one day play basketball for the West End High School Bluejays. Of course at an early age a child may also say they want to be a fireman because they like the red trucks. My goal was probably more serious than that, but it would not be truthful to say that it was an all consuming obsession, or that I spent long hours in the ice and snow working on a jump shot. I did play the game a lot starting in the fourth grade when we put a goal and net on the side of the detached garage. The garage, which rarely had a car in it, opened on to the alley behind our house which sat at the corner of 19th Avenue South and Belcourt Avenue. That meant that the side of the garage facing the yard was a solid wall although it did have a door that was never opened. Our large boxer dog Bill had a tendency to run away so the yard was completely fenced in and had a hedge about the same height as the fence. It was probably a four foot barrier and when it was first installed it was over my head and provided a real feeling of privacy.

Basketball wasn't the only game played in our back yard which was large enough to throw a baseball or kick a football the first few years we lived there. By the time my brother, who was two years older than me, reached junior high we had pretty much out grown the yard for anything more than a warm up location. The serious games were played on the Peabody College campus or after school on the Demonstration School grounds. There was no television in my childhood to look at and if I wasn't in school I was probably outside playing some kind of sport. If it was cold or raining I was probably inside reading a book. My paternal grandmother owned a retail bookstore and many of her presents came from the store. She was not someone to just hand one of her eight grandchildren a present without giving it some thought. If I got a book from her I knew I should read it because when I saw her she would ask me about it. It always seemed she was expecting me to read books at a slightly more adult level than my school required. Or maybe it was just that my brother and I tended to read the same books even though he was a little older. My grandmother was a major force in my life and I always enjoyed being around her. When I got older she even let me work at the bookstore during Christmas vacation. She had gone to college, somewhat rare in that time, and was the divorced mother of four children. The divorce might have been as rare as the college education for a woman in the South in the 1920s. She had a large interest in sports and would listen to the radio broadcast of the Nashville Vols, a minor league team, every night when she went to bed.

It was a simpler time in so many ways than today, but I don't like to romanticize it. It is true we didn't lock our doors with any regularity, but I didn't know my neighbors either, unless they had someone my age to play with. We had Negro maids who worked for little money and "carfare." The buses, restrooms, and water fountains were segregated and I would never have even thought about it if my parents hadn't been opposed to the practice. The only interaction I had with a child of a different color was the rare occasions when our maid Mattie would bring her son, Jo-Jo with her to work. We were told not to play in the front yard because "someone might see us." It was a simpler time, but not necessarily a better one.

The disappointing basketball season of the previous year made the prospects for the 1953-54 team uncertain at best. There were only three members from that team returning: French, Parsons, and Owens. Even though he had never played a minute of varsity basketball it was assumed that Greenbaum would be one of the starters. Beyond that there was a mixture of boys with B team experience and several seniors who had not even played on a B team who were trying out. I was in that category. The only blue and gray uniform I had ever worn was as a rarely used substitute on a bad junior high team three years earlier. My point total was six, all field goals, which came in the first three games. By the end of the season I didn't get into the game no matter how badly we were losing.

The negative experience of my junior high team was a distant memory and I was almost a foot taller, but not much heavier than I was at age fourteen. Actually there were two other members of that losing team competing for a spot on the varsity when practice began, John Niles, and Melvin Goldman. Melvin and I had played a lot, mostly against each other, in a league at the Jewish Community Center. We did both play on an all-star team one year and in a game against the Memphis all-stars, Melvin missed a free throw that I tipped in. It would be nice to say that was a game winner as the horn went off ending the game, but it was not. It did however come near the end of the game and kept us from falling behind in a game we eventually won.

The Center was a block from where we lived and we had a family membership from the day it opened. The fact that we were not Jewish was never a factor until it came time for the basketball all-star team to go to Memphis for a return game. The players would stay in homes and be expected to attend services, etc and it just wasn't a good idea for me to go because of possible charges that I was a "ringer," an outsider recruited for the team rather than a member of the center. The fact that I was indeed a member and played in that league for several years was not something I wanted to fight about. What was more important was whether that experience had improved my skills to the extent that Coach Shapiro would be impressed.

Apparently that was not going to be the case. I did make it to the final cut and Coach urged me to stay in shape in case something happened to any of the team members who remained. Melvin Goldman and John Niles were other first timers who were cut, but Archie Grant and Tommy Coke got the remaining spots. There was one academic casualty (Coke) at mid season, but all that did was reduce the squad from twelve to eleven. It stayed that way until the state tournament when you could only dress ten players when Jerry Morrison was cut. It would be an understatement to say I was disappointed, but an exaggeration to describe my feelings as devastated. I was given an opportunity and got to play a lot in a scrimmage against another school at the end of the first week. But, my primary skill on offense was an ability to shoot, rather than pass or handle the ball. On defense I was a good rebounder, more through positioning than leaping ability, but not much else. At an even six feet it didn't make sense to keep me when there were four others between 6'2 and 6'4 who were all juniors and had B team experience. Over the years the teenage disappointment has given way to the more adult realization that I must have been pretty good. I was one of the last people cut from a team that won a state championship.

The season started with a fairly predictable lineup. French and Greenbaum would be the guards with French serving as what we now call point guard. Greenbaum was not an inferior ball handler, it's just that he was more valuable as a mid to long range jump shooter. Besides French could dribble all day like Marques Haynes of the Harlem Globetrotters and no one could take the ball away from him. Because there was no shot clock this was a much more valuable skill than it would be today. The problem with the guard position was that they were both around five foot eight, and that might have been an exaggeration. Reserves Vaughn DuBose, Archie Grant, and Jerry Morrison weren't that much taller either. As the season wore on only DuBose got significant playing time.

At forward there was no real height either. Billy Owens was at best five foot eleven. He was usually assigned to guard the opposing team's best scorer. Buddy Parsons at the other forward spot was an unknown quantity when the season started. At six foot one he finally gave the team a little height and his ability to score points in streaks was well known, but how well he would mesh with the team's defensive philosophy was a mystery. There was a big void at center because Kenneth Zink had left school and joined the Air Force before his senior year. Initially the center spot went to Eddie Gaines at six foot four, but his tendency to foul meant he had to have a backup. Butch Stephens won that role and now the team was set for December with the nucleus consisting of a bunch of football players. They had a winning attitude carrying over from the fall, but no one was sure if that would translate to basketball.

Well apparently it did carry over as the Bluejays won eight straight games in December. Billy Owens was the high scorer with 17 points in the road opener against Central (46-41). He added 13 more in the next game at Howard (56-45), but Jimmy French got scoring honors with 19. Ralph Greenbaum got into the act with 21 at Lipscomb while French had 20 in the 72-56 victory. In the home opener French had 26 in a lopsided win over Springfield 73-37. The victory over Ryan was closer (51-45), but the balanced scoring continued between French (14), Greenbaum (12), and Owens (11). A formidable East team came to the West gym next, but while the favored Eagles led most of the game they faltered in the final quarter and West won 47-45. A surprise high scorer for the Blue Jays was Eddie Gaines with 15 points. The guard tandem of French (16) and Greenbaum (19) dominated the scoring in a road victory at North 64-37. As the Christmas holidays began the Bluejays remained undefeated by beating TIS 81-40. Buddy Parsons finally broke into double figures with 15 points. After a two week break West played an unscheduled game against a taller Hillsboro team. The Burros were still without a home court because of the fire at the school and the game was played at Central.

The first half was close with West leading 15-13 at the end of the first quarter. Hillsboro edged ahead at halftime 24-23, and increased their lead to 43-34 when the fourth quarter started. The final stanza was a battle between the tall Hillsboro center (Hatcher) who ended with 25 points and the smaller West guards. French had 16 and Greenbaum scored 17 in the comeback effort, but it was not enough. The undefeated string came to an end in a two point loss (48-50).

When the new year started there was certainly reason to be optimistic. The starting lineup was more or less set and all five players had shown an ability to score points. The lack of talent on the bench was a cause for concern, but it was obvious that if West stayed injury free they would be competitive with anyone remaining on the schedule.

A win at MBA (51-43) was followed by one over Clarksville (64-53). The next game with Cohn was closer (57-55) and a second game with Howard ended with almost the same score as the first (57-46). The return game with Lipscomb was even more lopsided than the first one as West won 63-39. The balanced scoring among the starters was continuing with Buddy Parsons beginning to show more offensive punch.

Just when you thought it couldn't get better it all came crashing down on January 22, 1954 when the Bluejays visited Father Ryan. The Irish stunned everyone by beating West 38-54. Ryan had a player named Joe Pat Breen who held Jimmy French scoreless that night for the only time in his junior high and high school career. Joe Pat later became Father Joseph Breen, but I first knew him as just another kid in the neighborhood long before high school. I will always remember him standing on the sidewalk outside our house with a basketball under his arm. He wouldn't come any closer because of our dog, but would yell for me or my brother to go up to Peabody College and play on the outdoor court. Because of a speech impediment he would pronounce my brother's name as "Bock." It was really Brock, but we knew what he meant.

Joe Pat and Jimmy French had been butting heads on the courts at Cavert for years before the scoreless game so close head to head competition was not a novelty to them. A major player in that game for Ryan was a sophomore called Louie Graham (13 points) who was their high scorer. Graham today is better known as golf pro Lou Graham, winner of the 1975 US Open. I played against Louie several times and never beat him at golf, but my brother did beat him in a tournament when Louie was a fourteen year old sensation. In addition to his ability as an athlete Lou Graham is one of the nicest people I have ever met. The same is true of Joe Pat Breen. If you're gonna lose it's nice to lose to people you like and respect.

West bounced back the next week with a lopsided victory over Hume-Fogg, 73-47 with all five starters scoring in double figures. That was expected and the real test would come on Friday night when West had to play at East High. They had barely beaten the Eagles in December, 47-45, and that was on the home court. The defeat wasn't as close as the two point loss to Hillsboro or as great as the sixteen point margin at Ryan, but it was a loss just the same. The final score of 48-54 made the game look closer than it actually was. West led all the way to the fourth quarter and then was outscored 15-6 in the final eight minutes. It was a long drive back across the river that night and people were really beginning to wonder how good this West High team really was.

Even with two straight Friday night losses the Jays still had a chance at being the top seeded team in the district tournament. The remaining six games were all rematches, except for Peabody which closed out the season. West won all six, but the margins were close enough to cause concern. They beat Cohn for the second time by only two points 56-54) and would probably be in the same bracket with them in the tournament. The games against MBA (51-46), Springfield (51-48), North (46-25), and TIS (49-34) were all victories, but each time by a lesser margin than the first game.

However, when you look at the season and compare it to others in recent years this team had definitely shown improvement. Their 19-3 record was Shapiro's best and similar to the numbers from the Strickland championship teams. The uncertainties about the squad at the beginning of the season had been answered in a positive manner. French was clearly a leader and his ball handling skills would be a test for any opponent. Greenbaum and Parsons had the ability to score points in amounts that might seem small today, but the average score by West that year was only 59 points. If you eliminate four one sided games where they scored over seventy points the average was 55. Billy Owens was a solid player and usually drew the toughest assignment on defense. However, he did contribute offensively with clutch shooting more than large numbers. By the end of the regular season Butch Stephens had become the starting center, but Eddie Gaines was still getting a lot of playing time. Gaines and Stephens were always undersized against the centers they opposed and other than the tendency to foul both had solid years. The only other players to get significant playing time were Vaughn DuBose and Eddie Greer. This team relied primarily on the starters who had been free of injuries all season fortunately. It was obvious also that this was a team that needed to get ahead or at least not get far behind because of the lack of offensive firepower.

It would be an exaggeration to say that anyone was predicting what was going to unfold over the next three weeks. West like all the other schools in the state had a lot of games to play before they could entertain any ideas of winning a state championship. There were no different classifications of schools back then so all the teams had a shot at winning the single state championship. That is, all the segregated white schools had that chance.

DISTRICT TOURNAMENT

As expected West was the top seeded team in the Eighteenth District tournament and had to play Cohn in the first game. The two regular season affairs had both been two point victories for the Bluejays and now they had to face a much taller Tiger team on a neutral floor. This time it was not the all white uniforms of the football team that made them "look bigger than they are," as Coach Shapiro had said before the season opener that ended in a scoreless tie. The Cohn starting lineup had three members the size of West's tallest player. As if Gary Gentry, Louis Green, and Charlie Fentress weren't enough, they could send in Jack Raby off the bench and hardly lose an inch. One thing West had going for them was they were a seeded team and this was their opening game. Cohn had not had a difficult time beating North in their opener, but this would be their second game in the tournament. For the tournament Coach

Shapiro added B Teamer Dallas Thomas to the roster which gave the Blue Jays some additional height, but no real increase in experience.

The other advantage West had in most games, even away from home or on a neutral court, was the enthusiasm of their fans. West High "school spirit" had been a phenomenon for years going back to the championship teams of Emmett Strickland. Heading into the Cohn game, and any that might follow, it was anticipated that loud, if not large, crowds would be the norm. There were a number of factors that contributed to the school spirit displayed by West. First of all it was, with a few exceptions, a middle class school and students, faculty, and parents had little trouble affording the modest prices charged for admission. Secondly, the teams were always interesting to watch even when they were not winning. When they were successful it was all the more interesting and people who might normally be quiet got caught up in the atmosphere. However, it was the 1954 team's ability to stay close or come from behind that made even the most cynical spectators excited.

Surprisingly Cohn fell easily, 71-44. The first quarter started slowly and ended with a 12-8 score that was hardly indicative of what was coming next. West led at the half 31-18 and maintained that lead at the end of the third quarter 43-31. In the fourth quarter Cohn lost their starting guard Junior Sullivan who fouled out and West was off to the races. For the night they took 62 shots to Cohn's total of 48. West shot what Jimmy Davy in the Tennessean reported as a "blistering" percentage of 37%. Looking back it appears that the difference in the number of shots taken was more of a factor than the percentage. Cohn shot 27% which was hardly blistering, but not that unusually low in 1954 high school basketball. West had their usual balanced scoring between Parsons (15), Owens (12), French (11) and Greenbaum (16). All eleven players saw action in the game with reserve guard Vaughn DuBose scoring eight points.

Needless to say the crowd was loud, but all this game did was set up a rematch with Father Ryan, one of the three losses West had in the regular season. If they won that game it might set up a rematch with East High, the last team to beat West that year. But that possibility was two days away and certainly lesser in importance than the Ryan game. The winner and the runner-up in the District tournament went to the Regional so just getting to the finals assured you of playing a little longer.

Back on West End Avenue the school spirit machine was beginning to gear up for the days ahead. West had a group of nine cheerleaders, three males and six females. They were selected after tryouts and were a mixture years before the concept of diversity was ever mentioned or even thought of. Four were holdovers from the previous year, two males, and two females. Four were seniors. Four were juniors and one was a sophomore. There were three that were Jewish which was about the only element of diversity possible in Nashville schools at that time. At least two of the females dated football players, but that apparently was not an automatic vote getter. They were cheerleaders simply because that was what they wanted to do and they brought a high level of organization and enthusiasm to the job. Of course the school had no women's sports at that time, except for tennis, which made cheerleading an outlet for a female interested in athletics. The motivation for the boys is harder to determine, but where they ended up as adults may give some helpful information. One became a preacher and insurance salesman, another became a politician, and the third is a lawyer. They obviously did not mind performing in public at an early age which may have steered them into their adult careers.

The cheerleaders relentlessly practiced their routines always lining up in their assigned spots. They actually led cheers and their audience was expected to know the words and yell them along with the leaders. This is a sharp contrast with today as cheering squads have actually become collections of gymnasts more for the entertainment of the crowd than the mundane task of actually leading a cheer. I find all the flips and pyramids of today distracting from the game itself.

As the tournaments progressed and West continued to win, the pep rallies, on school time, progressed from game day to every day. Athletes in some schools might have received some special consideration from sympathetic teachers, but if there was anybody getting by with outrageous behavior or skipping school I was not aware of it. The idea that someone would get a passing grade simply because they were a football or basketball player was unheard of. The main reasons for this I believe were Shapiro would not stand for it and sports were simply one of many facets in these boy's lives. Most intended to go to college, and did, although only four played basketball at that level. There were some teachers who were more outspoken in their love of the athletic tradition at the school than others, but I don't remember anyone who was openly critical of it. Sometimes it did get in the way of education. There was one particular math teacher who truly bled blue and grey and students were always trying to get her to talk about a recent game or the upcoming one. This attempt to avoid the rigors of algebra or geometry had mixed results, but there certainly were classes where the full period was not used for instruction. There was a lot that was different from today. Television was just beginning in Nashville with one NBC channel to start with. The World Series was played in the afternoon. Doc was enough of a baseball fan that he would play the World Series games over the school intercom so students could listen if the teacher allowed it. I don't know about other classes, but the algebra teacher always let it play. Her interest in athletics apparently went beyond our little school.

The head cheerleader was a slender boy named Gene Rutledge, known for boundless enthusiasm and energy. Gene delighted in coming up with new ways to enthuse crowds and some of his ideas got mixed results. At one point in the tournament he decided it would be a good way to start the game by having the team burst through a paper display as they took the court. The problem with the idea was building a frame strong enough to hold the paper required a fairly large amount of wood. When the paper was attached it was a lot heavier than it appeared. A cheerleader had to hold the frame on each side firmly enough so it wouldn't fall to the floor when Jimmy French, basketball in hand, raced onto the court. The paper had to be strong enough to accommodate a water color picture of a Bluejay, or whatever design was arrived at before the game. The four foot wide and six foot tall painted structure had to dry and be transported to the Lipscomb gym. Then someone had to convince the gatekeepers to allow it inside. But, who could turn down six attractive young ladies accompanied by a future preacher, lawyer, and politician?

Gene not only orchestrated these tasks, he even convinced the Lipscomb facility manager to dim the lights and allow a spotlight as the show started. That only happened once and was roundly criticized by many people, including Edgar Allen, the Banner reporter. It really was a little excessive and the West High antics over the years had been an irritation to a lot of people. The changing picture and reusable frame continued, but the lights stayed on thereafter.

None of this was going to matter if Joe Pat Breen held Frenchie scoreless and the Irish beat West again. This game was a low scoring affair and West held a two point lead, 29-27, when the fourth quarter started. Greenbaum scored eight points in the last period and French didn't miss a shot the last eight minutes. The final score was 47-36 and between them the two West High guards had scored 27 of the team's points. Joe Pat Breen was held to seven points and going home, but before that he was the high scorer in the consolation game against East with 16 points. Breen was the high scorer for the tournament with 47 in three games.

Individual honors did not matter to the players that much. They were just happy to be going to the Regional tournament. However, the rematch with East was not going to happen because MBA upset the Eagles 52-45. And so it developed that two of the Nashville schools advancing to the Regional tournament, which would also be held at the Lipscomb gym, were just blocks apart on West End Avenue. West had already defeated the Big Red three times that year, once in football and twice in basketball. All the games were close, but nothing compared to what happened in the final game.

The phenomenon of school spirit at West High had a musical component that further set it apart from other schools. It started innocently enough in 1948 when a lone student with a trumpet played the song "I'm Looking Over A Four Leaf Clover" and the crowd, of course knowing the words, started singing along. The words have absolutely nothing to do with basketball, West High, or really much of anything.

"I'm looking over a four leaf clover that I overlooked before.
One leaf is sunshine, the second is rain,
Third is the roses that grow in the lane.
No need explaining the one remaining is somebody I adore.
I'm looking over a four leaf clover that I overlooked before."

Most students sang the words while others sang a more risqué version they had adapted containing various references to female anatomy. Whether the words made sense or needed to be censored it gave the high school a song to sing. A lot of rhythmic clapping and a loud trumpet drowned out the words anyway.

The song was written in 1927 by two well known writers. Harry Woods (1896-1970) wrote the music and Mort Dixon (1892-1956) the lyrics. Woods wrote several other tunes including "When The Red, Red Robin Comes Bob, Bob, Bobbing Along"; "When the Moon Comes Over the Mountain"; and "Try A Little Tenderness." I do not know if he ever realized a high school in Tennessee was playing his song, and I doubt if there were ever any royalties paid to ASCAP or BMI. But technically speaking it was a copywrited song being played before a paying audience. Maybe he was more interested in counting the money that came in after Otis Redding resurrected "Try A little Tenderness." Or perhaps he had already retired on the income from Kate Smith singing "When The Moon Comes Over The Mountain." Mort Dixon made it to the Songwriters Hall of Fame, but not exclusively for Four Leaf Clover. He also wrote "That Old Gang of Mine"; "Bye, Bye, Blackbird"; and "I Found a Million Dollar Baby". Four Leaf Clover received very little attention until 1948 when it was recorded by Art Mooney and went to number one in the Billboard charts. After 1948 it received little attention, other than at West End High School in Nashville, Tennessee.

By 1954 the lone trumpeter had evolved into a band, if you can call four or five people a band. Their repertoire consisted of more than the fight song, if you want to say the bland lyrics of Four Leaf Clover constituted a "fight song." Because they had played at all the football games these musicians could open a game with the "Star Spangled Banner" and end it with the Alma Mater. The Alma Mater wasn't original either. It was simply the Vanderbilt song substituting the three words "West End High" for the three syllables in Vanderbilt. Both songs start out with the phrase "On the city's western border," which was literally true for Vanderbilt in 1907 when Robert Vaughn wrote the words to the song. It was true for West in 1937 as well, but it sounds a little strange today when the western border of Nashville is the Davidson County line.

In the interest of full disclosure it has to be acknowledged that the song is not original to Vanderbilt either, and is used by numerous other schools. It originated in Cornell in 1875. The words by Archibald Weeks and Wilmot Smith were added to a tune written in 1857 by H.S. Thompson. There are no references to cities or western borders in the Cornell version. It begins with "Far Above Cayuga's waters," a reference to Lake Cayuga near Ithaca, New York.

Loud cheers and music were nice, but the game would have to be won on the floor. MBA could develop a fair amount of enthusiasm because virtually every student at the all male school attended their games, and often recent alumni would show up in large numbers. The school had to import female cheerleaders from other schools. They all came from all girl schools as far as I could tell which makes sense. It would not add to a student's popularity if she was, for instance, attending Hillsboro and seen leading cheers for an opposing team. But, regardless of who won the noise battle, the loser of this game was facing a difficult path in the Regional tournament the following week. They would have to play Hillsboro, a surprise loser to Donelson in the 19th District Tournament. The winner of that game would face Woodlawn one of the top rated teams in the state.

West did win, but it was one of the closest and most exciting games in their long tournament history. The 61-57 victory added another District championship trophy to go with the six others that were already in the lobby of the school. The first quarter started slowly and the score was tied 6-6 after the first eight minutes. The tempo of the game picked up slightly before halftime with West leading 17-15. The MBA center, Carlin Rolfe had made nine of his team's points in that half.

After the intermission both teams continued the cautious play that had characterized the first half. Neither team had a deep bench so it was important to avoid foul trouble. But, obviously West had to contain Rolfe to win the game. He was held to one shot in the third quarter which ended with MBA clinging to a one point lead, 29-28. With four minutes to go West had worked their way to a three point lead, but three foul shots by Jimmy Martin put MBA back into a tie 34-34. French and Greenbaum controlled the ball for most of the low scoring final quarter which was the type of strategy that would lead to a shot clock in later years. But, this was 1954 and West fans loved to watch Frenchie go into his dribbling act and the opposing team and fans hated it. It worked all the way down to the final minute when West called a time out. Again French and Greenbaum worked the ball until seven seconds remained and French took an off balance jump shot which missed.

In the first overtime period neither team scored. MBA got off one shot and West missed two. The second overtime had no fixed time period. Teams just played until someone scored which was called sudden death. It certainly looked like death to the Bluejays when MBA controlled the tip. However, Bobby Calton missed the shot and the Big Red didn't get set up on defense as French weaved in and out of defenders and put in a game winning six foot jump shot.

Joe Shapiro was going to the Regional tournament for the second time in three years. West had balanced scoring for the tournament from the three seniors. Greenbaum had 35 points, Owens 34, and French 31. French was selected as the most outstanding player in a vote that was surely delayed until the final gun on the final night. If it had been determined earlier and awarded to someone else the crowd would certainly have been amazed, and probably angry. French and Greenbaum made the all-tournament team along with Breen, and two MBA players, Carlin Rolfe and Dickie Anderson. Selecting Anderson over Owens was certainly questionable because Owens guarded the MBA star in the final game and held him scoreless while making 14 points himself.

REGIONAL TOURNAMENT

     Monday March 1, 1954 was a busy news day in the world and the United States. America announced that it had successfully tested a hydrogen bomb in the Pacific atoll of Bikini. This bomb was said to be even more powerful than the two atomic bombs that had been dropped on Japan at the end of World War II. Meanwhile in Washington, DC, four Puerto Rican extremists opened fire in the House of Representatives wounding five people before being subdued by capitol police. If anyone at West End High was aware of these two events they did not mention it. Most students were looking forward to the assembly program that morning and the presentation to the school of the basketball trophy won the previous weekend.

     It was an emotional occasion as the possibility of going further than these students had ever experienced was beginning to look like something that could happen. The winning tradition at the school probably meant more to outside observers than it did to the team members. They were all in the fifth or sixth grade when West won their last championship in 1948. But, Dr. Yarbrough did remember the past success and so did Coach Shapiro although he was coaching at other schools then. Jimmy French as captain presented the trophy to Doc and got too emotional to continue speaking. Doc tried to reassure Frenchie and anyone else who was paying attention that it was only a game and what was important was doing your best. Losing an athletic contest was hardly the worst thing that could happen to you in life, but try telling that to a teenager. Coach Shapiro just looked like he was concerned his star player was getting too intense and needed to relax and take things as they came. Anyway there were two days to kill until the next game with Donelson.

Even though Donelson was a Davidson County school we didn't really know anything about them. To my knowledge we never played them in any sport and although they weren't that far away in distance it wasn't a quick trip to the community south of Nashville. Donelson was named for the wife of Andrew Jackson, Rachel Donelson, and was a suburban community between the Nashville Airport and the Cumberland River. In later years when the interstate highways were completed and Old Hickory Dam was built on the Cumberland River there was a lot of housing development in the area. When Percy Priest Dam was built on the Stones River and the airport expanded the area grew even more rapidly and farmland virtually disappeared.

The opening game in this tournament was certainly different from a scouting perspective than the District tournament had been. In the previous week West played three teams they had already seen twice during the regular season. This week they were playing a team they had never seen, but they did know the Dons had beaten Hillsboro in the 19th District tournament. Hillsboro was one of three teams that beat West in the regular season and the only one of the three still alive in the tournament.

The game got off to a predictably slow start with West leading 10-7 at the end of the first quarter. The second quarter wasn't any more exciting offensively and West had a one point lead at halftime (17-16). The second half was more of the same, but unfortunately for West several players were in foul trouble and it appeared the heretofore unused bench was going to see action. But, the Jays were still ahead by one (30-29) when the fourth quarter started. Scorers on both sides came alive and West trailed Donelson 46-44 as the clock wound down and when play ended it appeared the Dons were a two point winner. The dream of a fourth state championship was going to be denied and it had been a hard game against a good team.

But a foul was called as time expired and Ralph Greenbaum had a chance to go to the line and put his team into overtime for the second straight game. All he had to do was make both free throws…easier said than done. How many times have athletes in the backyard or on the playground put themselves in the imaginary position of potential game winners, even providing the play-by-play commentary as they take their shots? In my lifetime I have seen or heard that scenario hundreds of times, but it was always a chance to WIN the game. This time it was simply a matter of making two, not one, shots to avoid losing. Truth may or may not be stranger than fiction, but in this case truth was making for an interesting story.

Because the game was actually over the clock showed zero and Greenbaum was at the free throw line by himself when the official, Julius "Rock" Sneed handed him the ball. To the official's amazement Greenbaum said "these are precious, aren't they?" Then he made both efforts as if he was just winding up a practice session. Donelson was stunned. The game they thought they had won was back to square one. Instead of taking a shower they were going back on the court for a three minute overtime. It is probably fortunate that Sneed was the official who handed Greenbaum the ball at the foul line. The other official, Hickman Duncan, was as loquacious as Ralph and they might still be standing there talking today.

There was more clutch free throw shooting by the Bluejays, but this time it was from Vaughn Dubose a reserve guard. Foul trouble had forced Shapiro into a small lineup as both centers fouled out and Bobby Glenn, a rarely used substitute saw some action. When the first overtime ended in a 50-50 tie, West was heading to a second consecutive sudden death overtime. This time it was over quickly. Greenbaum assumed the taller Dons would control the center jump and deflect the ball to one of their guards. It happened just the way he envisioned and he jumped in front of the Donelson player who didn't go to meet the ball. The tip fell in his hands and he drove in for the winning layup all alone. The following night MBA upset Hillsboro. Now fans were wondering if the Maroons would get another shot at West in the finals of the Regional. First

MBA had to beat Woodlawn and that would be a major upset. All West had to do to get to their first State Tournament since 1948 was defeat McEwen, a team most students had never heard of and couldn't locate on a map.

McEwen is one of those small towns that travelers from Nashville to Memphis went through before Interstate 40 created a lot of ghost towns. The same West End Avenue that is the address of Vanderbilt University and West End High School continues westerly and becomes Harding Road and about eight miles from the Cumberland River where it started as Broadway splits into two distinctly different highways. The northern route, or Highway 70 was a better highway, but it went through several small towns which made for slow going. The southern alternative was Highway 100 which had several twists and turns, but very few towns of any size. Either way you did it you were in for a five to six hour drive and you needed to fill up with food and gasoline before you left Nashville. This was especially true if you took the scenic southern Highway 100 route. In West Tennessee the two highways came together at Jackson and continued on to Memphis.

McEwen was a small town on Highway 70 and they made it to the Regional tournament as runner-up to Woodlawn, the acknowledged powerhouse in the field. When they went on defense their cheerleaders would chant "git the ball, git the ball, git it, git it" to the delight of the crowd. It was probably a form of urban snobbishness, but ---as the game went on the West high fans started chanting the same cheer. In retrospect it was probably not one of our prouder moments, but at least I do know where that particular cheer originated.

I am less certain when a Gene Rutledge yell of "shout chillun! Shout hallelulah" started, but it was certainly an indicator of the profession the future Baptist minister would enter later. All of this systematic cheering and yelling added to the image of West End High School as a school with enormous "school spirit." Blue and grey tassels on the end of foot long dowels were in most hands and were always in motion as the band played Four Leaf Clover and other tunes throughout the games. The only time the crowd would grow quiet was when the opposing team shot a foul shot. In the 1950s it was customary for everyone to get quiet when a player went to the foul line. Coach Shapiro thought it was unnerving to go from a frenzied crowd to near silence at such a time. He encouraged West fans to keep on making noise when we were shooting fouls, but act like they were at a funeral when the other team was at the line. I don't know if anyone ever studied how effective this practice was, but it was such a break from established decorum many were surprised when the Blue Jay fans began the practice.

It would be nice if I could say that the team and its fans had dedicated the season to Dr. Yarbrough weeks before they found themselves one game away from going back to the state tournament for the first time in six years. But, the truth is the cheer "All The Way For Doc" started well into the tournament journey and actually originated spontaneously at a pep rally at the school. There is more than one opinion about when that happened, but whenever it was it just happened and no one person can claim to be the originator. At any rate for the remainder of the tournament it became the primary chant, leaving the old standby "West is Best," as well as "git the ball" and "shout chillun" well behind in frequency. It became something the crowd would start rather than being led by the cheerleaders who had a more carefully choreographed idea of the game. Variety and style points were out the window for the West partisans; they were ready to win. But, they almost didn't.

The headline on Saturday morning, March 6, 1954 said "West, Woodlawn Roar Into State." Certainly Woodlawn did "roar" by destroying MBA 70-54 in a game that was never close. But, West struggled to beat McEwen by one point, 42-41. McEwen was a taller team, but West took a 16-7 lead in the first quarter. The lead didn't hold up and West had only a two point lead at halftime (24-22). McEwen went ahead 34-33 in the third quarter and the game remained even until the last two minutes and fifteen seconds of the game. With West leading 40-39 Jimmy French went into his dribbling routine until he was fouled at the 1:35 mark. He made both foul shots and the score went to 42-39. A late goal by McEwen made it a one point victory for the Blue Jays. The game was supposed to be a breeze for West, but it was so close that only six players saw action. The following night it was expected West would be beaten by a taller team from Woodlawn, but it wouldn't matter because both teams were in the sixteen team field for the state tournament at the recently completed Vanderbilt Memorial Gymnasium.

If you think McEwen was a small town, try finding Woodlawn. First of all there are six towns in Tennessee with that name in the following counties: Cumberland, Greene, Loudon, Montgomery, Washington, and Wayne. The undefeated (24-0) team that came to the Regional tournament was from Montgomery County and had an enrollment of 85 students. Ten of them played basketball and five were over six feet tall. But, the main attraction was a 6'4" senior named Lawrence Gibbs. "Lonzo" Gibbs was an all star performer and a true college prospect.

West started out hot and never looked back as they beat the favored Bulldogs 62-45, the largest margin of victory since the District tournament opener with Cohn. West shot 41% for the game and jumped into an early 20-9 lead after one quarter. They cooled off in the second quarter, but still led 28-17 at halftime. Woodlawn was still within striking distance when the final quarter started and only trailed 39-29. But, the balanced scoring of Jimmy French (11), Ralph Greenbaum (12), Buddy Parsons (14), and Billy Owens (17) was more than enough to seal the win. For the game Lonzo Gibbs only scored 11 points and was held scoreless in the second half. French, Greenbaum, and Parsons all made the all tournament team, leaving Billy Owens to wonder what he would have to do to get such an honor. For the second week in a row he had played solid offense while guarding a taller opponent and holding them below their season average. But, this was a team victory and in all the years I knew Billy Owens I never heard him complain about any personal slights he might have suffered. He knew what his role was on this team and he performed it. It might go unrecognized in the news media, but his coach, teammates, and knowledgeable fans were well aware of his contribution. Besides, the goal was to get to the state tournament and that was the next stop.

WEST-PETERSBURG, MARCH 10

The final goal was now in sight for a basketball team that played well all season and consistently exceeded the expectations of both their fans and their critics. Even the objective reporters who covered them from the start, Jimmy Davy of the Tennessean and Edgar Allen of the Banner, did not feel the Blue Jays were a favorite to win the state tournament when it started. At least they did not say so in print, perhaps because both had official roles to play in the tournament. Allen would run the time clock and Davy was the official scorer.

The tournament was being held at the Vanderbilt gym which had opened in 1952. At that time it had a seating capacity of 6,583 which made it the largest facility in the state. The school was obviously eager to make a good impression with its new facility to the sixteen teams playing in the tournament. The format for the week was different from some of the earlier ones that West had won. This time there was no playoff system to determine as many as eight spots in the final ranking. If you lost a game before the semi finals you went home, but there would be a consolation game for third and fourth place on the final night. The geographical diversity was evident with teams coming from the far ends of the state. Memphis Treadwell was from the southwest and two teams came from the northeast corner, Kingsport and Johnson City. Dyersburg was almost to the Kentucky border in the northwest part of the state and Bradley County was in the southeast part of the state where Tennessee, Georgia, and North Carolina converge. Other than Treadwell, West was the only school from a major city in the tournament. Sleeping in your own bed and eating home cooked meals might provide some advantage, but very few of the West players had ever been on the unusual configuration of Memorial Gym before the first game with Petersburg.

There has been a lot of criticism about the layout of the Vanderbilt facility in recent years, but if you look at history there were valid reasons for the design in the early 1950s. After World War II came to an end there were twelve schools in the Southeastern Conference (SEC), although they were not the same twelve schools as today. Tulane and Georgia Tech were members back then. Arkansas and South Carolina joined later. The only school in the conference that played serious basketball was the University of Kentucky and UK was also the only school with a large facility on campus. When Vanderbilt decided to challenge Kentucky in basketball it was obvious that a spacious facility would be necessary in order to recruit players and develop a fan base. However, the cost of such a building was a factor so it had to be a place that would be used for more than 12-15 home basketball games a year. This led to the two features that are most criticized: (1) the benches at the end of the court instead of on the sidelines, and (2) the first rows of seats below the playing surface on the sidelines. But there were valid reasons at the time for these decisions.

In order to use the building for physical education classes (male only at the time), a floor was constructed that was large enough to accommodate three basketball courts which would run north and south. In the center, running east and west would be the court used for actual games. The end zone seats had a rollaway feature that allowed for the three courts, but when extended provided the closest seats to the action. But, this meant that the permanent seats on both sides were not as close to the sidelines as most arenas are today. It's a mixed blessing in my opinion. Having gone to a high school where you ran into a brick wall that was three feet from the sideline, it was nice to play somewhere you could run full speed after a loose ball and not worry about getting hurt. The benches at the end of the court actually came about a few years after construction, but that didn't seem to be that big a deal either because that's where they were in the West high gym. In fact both teams had their bench under the same goal.

But, initially the benches were on the sidelines and slightly below the playing surface as were the first several rows on both sides. The north side had chair back seats and was primarily for season ticket holders. The south side was the student section with bench type seats. At that time there was no facility in Nashville suitable for public performances and large meetings. That is hard to believe today when Nashville abounds with football stadiums, hockey arenas, symphony halls, and other facilities, but at that time only the Ryman Auditorium and War Memorial auditorium were available. The Ryman was home to the Grand Ole Opry on weekends, so any traveling shows had to play there during the week. The War Memorial (World War I) was home to the Nashville Symphony and numerous high school graduations. The plan was for the north side of the Vanderbilt Memorial Gym (World War II) to be used for performances other than basketball, hence the lowered seats in the front and the theatre-like gradual rise of the remainder. It was a good idea, but other than Vanderbilt assemblies and graduations (when it rained) it never materialized.

As years went by balconies were added on the north side (1965) and then the south side (1967). This increased the seating capacity to over 10,000. The demand for tickets was high because the team was consistently competitive and local players like Clyde Lee and Perry Wallace elected to attend the school. In 1969 the end zones added balconies bringing the total to almost 15,000 seats. Until 1992 the facility was still a "no-frills" place with unpainted block walls and plain concrete floors in the lobbies. Another renovation led to painted walls and a black and gold motif throughout the building. Realizing the end zone seats could be sold at a premium the rollaway sections were replaced with chair backs which decreased seating capacity slightly, but added revenue. Today the gym hardly looks like it did when I was in school, but it still has the same feel and atmosphere it had in 1954.

The first games were played on Tuesday, March 9th, but instead of four games there were only three, all played in the afternoon. That night there was an SEC playoff game between Kentucky and LSU to determine the conference championship because both teams had identical records. At that time only one team from a conference went to the NCAA tournament so the game had added significance. The SEC tournament once determined the conference champion, but the tournament was discontinued after Vanderbilt beat Kentucky in 1951. Kentucky had several star players who would later play in the NBA like Frank Ramsey, Cliff Hagen, and Lou Tsiouropilis. LSU was led by Bob Pettit who went on to a long career with the St. Louis (later Atlanta) Hawks where ironically he teamed with Hagan. Ramsey and Tsiouropilis played professionally with the Boston Celtics. The Wildcats won 63-56 before a crowd estimated at 7,500 which was larger than the seating capacity of the gym. The attendance for the three high school games that afternoon was announced at 1,235. After winning the playoff game Kentucky elected not to go to the NCAA tournament after all so LSU represented the conference. The announced reason UK declined was certainly convoluted. At that time the eligibility rules for the NCAA were more stringent than they were for the SEC. The SEC allowed a player to have three years of eligibility over a longer period than the NCAA. This meant the three star players for Kentucky, Hagen, Ramsey, and Tsiouropilis, who had sat out a year when UK was on probation, could not play in the tournament. Obviously their ineligibility was known before the game so why did they insist on playing it? Was it simply an opportunity to showcase the Blue and White before fans from Middle Tennessee and Southern Kentucky and pick up a check in the process. Whatever it was it made some extra money for Vanderbilt and made the scheduling of early games in the state tournament more difficult. Because my parents had season tickets to Vanderbilt home games I got to go to the game with my father. There were certainly a lot more UK fans in the gym than LSU.

The next day it was necessary to play five games to make up for the lost evening session. The afternoon attendance was a little higher than the day before at 1,506, but nothing like the packed house for the college game. The evening session drew 2,249 when the local team took the floor for their opener against Petersburg at 9:30 PM. The Petersburg Bulldogs were one of those small schools, enrollment 110, that disappeared after desegregation and consolidated schools began to dominate rural county school districts. Needless to say Coach Shapiro knew nothing about the team he was playing and their regular season record was not impressive (12-5). They did have more height than the Bluejays, but that was a situation they had faced all year. Participants in the state tournament were only allowed ten players so Jerry Morrison and Dallas Thomas traded their seats on the bench for ones in the stands.

Perhaps it was the lateness of the start, but the game was a lot closer than anticipated and West escaped with a 51-43 victory. At the end of the first quarter West led by seven points (10-3) and 26-15 at halftime. With a lead of 41-28 after three quarters it looked like an easy victory. Unfortunately they were outscored in the fourth quarter, but it was not enough for a Petersburg comeback. Edgar Allen described the Bulldogs as "scrappy." And Jimmy Davy said West "sputtered past Petersburg." West was able to use nine players in the game with Archie Grant making a rare appearance. Now it was one down and three to play and an excellent Lake City team was the next obstacle to face less than 24 hours after the first victory.

The first two days of play had reduced the field to eight and five regional champions had lost. Woodlawn, the team that West beat in the regional tournament, was very impressive in their 84-59 victory over Bolton. There were two players in the field who would later meet on the football field when Vanderbilt played Tennessee. Phil King made an early exit as Dyersburg lost to Linden 61-50. King would be a star halfback for the Commodores and then played in the NFL for the New York Giants and Pittsburgh Steelers. Jim Smelcher went on to play at UT, but for now he was a big part of a talented Lake City team facing West in their Thursday night game.

WEST-LAKE CITY,
MARCH 11

For a change West faced a team that was not as tall as the
Bluejays, but not by a lot. All eight teams remaining in the

tournament had impressive season and tournament records. Kingsport was one of three teams from East Tennessee, and the other two came from the same district (Lake City and LaFollette). Middle Tennessee was represented by West, Linden, Woodlawn, and McMinn County. The only team west of the Tennessee River was Treadwell from Memphis. The home court advantage for West was in full gear as the next game approached. Vanderbilt authorities imposed no restrictions on the Blue Jay fans so the band had expanded to more than four members now wearing their uniforms. It was a busy week for the band members who in addition to attending school and performing at the games were also preparing for the musical equivalent of a state tournament. The pregame ritual of bursting through a banner was expanded by having two majorettes holding the sides of the display. A picture in the Banner shows the cheerleaders and majorettes in their uniforms which are a far cry from the more scantily clad versions of today. It is also a sign of the times to see the uniforms worn by the players. The shorts were truly short, but often knee high socks were worn and in some cases, but not West, players had knee pads. West had a mix and match approach from game to game. Against Petersburg it was an all blue combination, but Lake City got the all white version.

By the time the West-Lake City game started three more teams had been eliminated in the earlier games. Before 1,321 fans Kingsport beat Linden and Lafollette beat Woodlawn in the afternoon setting up an East Tennessee semi final game. Attendance was higher that evening (1,887) when Treadwell beat McMinn County, but it was lower than the night before by 20%. Those who stayed away missed some exciting games. Woodlawn lost by one point in overtime and the Kingsport and Treadwell victories were each by one point. So what could top that? West got to play another overtime game and pulled put a four point victory, 46-42.

The opponent was Lake City, a small town in East Tennessee in Anderson County. The town was originally called Coal Creek and was the scene of a bitter dispute between coal miners and coal company owners in the late 19th century over the use of prison labor. The practice was outlawed by the Tennessee legislature and in 1896 the state built a prison in adjoining Morgan County which also was a coal mine. The maximum security facility at Petros,

Tennessee, called Brushy Mountain is still in use today and has housed some of the most famous convicts in history, including James Earl Ray. Ray actually escaped from the prison in 1977, but was unable to get over the mountains wedged against the facility.

The stream that runs through Lake City is still called Coal Creek, but the city name was changed after the TVA built Norris Dam which created a large lake nearby. Anderson County is better known for the city of Oak Ridge, home of the Oak Ridge National Laboratory and the birthplace of the atomic bomb in World War II. Even though the towns of Lake City and Oak Ridge are 21 miles apart it takes almost forty minutes to drive between them, because of the hilly terrain. The drive takes you through the county seat of Clinton which would become famous a few years later in 1956 when riots occurred after the schools were ordered to integrate. The minority population of the county was so small at that time Negro students had to attend segregated Austin High School in Knoxville which was 35 miles away and an hour's drive.

But, all of this past and future history was lost on the players and fans of the two schools as the game approached. While West had a home court advantage that was growing with each game it was not translating into a belief that the Bluejays should be favored to win the tournament. Edgar Allen described them as a "question mark" that "slopped through" the Petersburg game. He made Lake City a favorite to win, while the Litratings service showed West as a four point favorite. The state tournament was beginning to take over the sports pages of both papers, partly because a local team was still alive, but also because of the absence of any other sports news at the moment. In 1954 there was no March Madness with three weeks of NCAA college tournament basketball and about all people in Nashville knew about that tournament was the University of Kentucky had won it several times. Actually they had won it three times, 1948, 1949, and 1951, but they were not going to play this year even though they had defeated LSU for the conference championship in a playoff game earlier that week. The NCAA ruled several UK players as ineligible (Hagen, Ramsey, and Tsioropoulus) so LSU represented the SEC after all as reported earlier.

It was another late night start on a school night and the fact that students might not get home until almost midnight could have had an effect on the attendance. A bigger factor might have been the radio broadcasts of Larry Munson who had only been in Nashville a few years at the time. Munson had a flair for the dramatic which had been put to the test in the first part of his career when he would broadcast Nashville Vols road baseball games by Western Union "re-creation." In those games he would be in a radio studio with an audio engineer receiving a teletype account of the game which was sketchy at best. Between him and his engineer he would intersperse crowd noise and even the crack of the bat which was said to be done by hitting a pencil against a block of wood on his desk. Whatever the method was he had a flair for making the games from afar sound the same as when he sat in the press box at Sulpher Dell ballpark. Unfortunately an off color remark made when he thought the microphone was dead almost ended his career. But, the local fans felt it was simply a youthful mistake and many wrote letters urging his reinstatement. One of the letter writers was my grandmother who went to sleep most nights in the summer listening to the broadcast of the Nashville Vols baseball team.

Any earlier indiscretions were long forgotten by the time the 1954 tournament rolled around and Munson had been doing high school football and basketball games for several years and was familiar with the local history. The three week march through opposition by the "undersized Blue Jays and their two midget guards" was made to order for his approach. For over fifty years I have heard people talk about those games as if they were there in person, but I have a hunch many of them were either listening to Munson or reading what Allen and Davy had to say.

West was not a particularly hard team to scout even in the abbreviated time of a sixteen team tournament. The two guards would handle the ball with French being what today would be called a "point guard" and Greenbaum a "two" or "shooting guard." They were listed in the program as 5'7" (French) and 5'8" (Greenbaum) which wasn't all that different than the Lake City Guards who were 5'7" (Mac Hill) and 5'11" (Bobby Leach. The Blue Jays had balanced scoring between the two guards and two forwards (Parsons and Owens), but the main reason it was balanced was they actually scored so few points. The close games so far had been low scoring affairs and Lake City was not going to be any different. Tough defense was the key to this team, but by March 11th that wasn't a secret anymore.

The first period was close and West trailed 13-11. They came back to lead 23-21 at halftime and 32-30 when the fourth quarter began. The Lakers tied the game with 4:15 left and then went ahead 41-39 as time was running out. Lake City had played an excellent game up to that point and proceeded to make a number of mistakes that put the Jays back in it. Even though Bobby Leach was three inches taller Ralph Greenbaum blocked his shot out of bounds. The throw in pass went out of bounds to no one and West had the ball with nineteen seconds left. What came next was certainly predictable, but not pretty. French drove the length of the floor and put up a shot that missed. The rebound came right back to the little guard and this time the shot went down, but there were a few bounces on the rim before it settled in. How many times it bounced before tying the score depends on how dramatic the many eye (and ear) witnesses want to make it. There are no video or audio records to establish the truth, but as someone who was there I can truthfully say I thought the game was lost three times in the last minute!

The overtime was not nearly as interesting as the game had been. Greenbaum made two free throws, French stole the ball for an uncontested layup, and Buddy Parsons added a foul shot. Lake City only scored one point in the overtime, a free throw by Leach. For the game, French had 15 points, Greenbaum 12, and Parsons 10. But, the most unlikely hero of the game was reserve center Eddie Gaines, the only substitute in the game, with seven points and a number of clutch rebounds before fouling out. Next stop: Memphis Treadwell winners of a close game against McMinn County.

WEST-TREADWELL, MARCH 12

For the first time since the Donelson game in the regional tournament West was playing a team from a city they could find on a map. But, they couldn't tell you where the school was in the Shelby County town that was at that time the largest city in the state. Actually the school is in an area close to downtown and at that time did not have a particularly illustrious athletic history. In later years it was known as the high school of Anfernee "Penny" Hardaway who played at Memphis State (now called University of Memphis) and various teams in the NBA. But, in 1954 all we knew was they had beaten a couple of teams, Johnson City and McMinn County, who were good enough to make the state tournament. They must be pretty good and were certainly taller than the Blue Jays. They also had a larger enrollment (800) than West (503), but whether that meant a large contingent of fans would make the trip for the weekend games remained to be seen. It was more likely fans would be attracted to the 7:30 game between Kingsport and LaFollette. That contest was for the mythical championship of that part of the state. When the tournament began it was expected the eventual champion would come from one of the four teams from upper East Tennessee, Johnson City, Kingsport, Lake City, or Lafollette. There was still a fifty percent chance of that happening.

The story line on West continued to cast them as underdogs and Edgar Allen described them as "weary" in the afternoon paper before the Treadwell game. The news coverage was now becoming an all out full court effort. The sports editors of the papers rarely mentioned high school athletics in their columns, but Fred Russell led off his Banner "Sidelines" with a tribute to Dr. Yarbrough and the emotion behind the cheer "All The Way For Doc." He wrote "I don't know of a school man in the world who is held in deeper affection by his boys and girls than is Dr. Yarbrough." That was certainly the case in my family. Doc had been the principal at Peabody Demonstration School when my mother was a student there. My cousins and my older brother preceded me at West and they never had anything bad to say about him. I certainly had a high regard for him and a lot of reasons to be grateful. First, he allowed me to attend West in the ninth grade although I actually lived in the Cavert School district. We planned to move into an apartment in the West zone in December so he allowed me to register from my grandmother's address in that same apartment building.

This meant I got to take my freshman algebra class from Doc himself who always liked to teach at least one class. Because he taught a math class I always assumed that was his primary field of interest. But, in researching this book I found that his main area was history and he had written at least one book on the region. He had some unorthodox teaching methods to say the least, but there were things I learned from him in that class (besides algebra) that I used years later when I became a teacher myself. Doc loved to tell jokes, but they had a purpose. One of my favorites was the story about the Army cook who had 100 eggs to fry for 100 soldiers. The night before the breakfast he broke one of the eggs and he spent the rest of the night deciding which soldier to kill. The moral might have escaped many in the class, but I took away the following lesson. A mathematical solution to a problem may solve the problem, but it is not always a happy solution.

Another trick Doc liked to use was he would come to class and put a problem on the blackboard. Then he would put a quarter on his desk and say the first person with the correct solution would get the quarter. It might have been improper, but it motivated a lot of students, especially so-called tough guys, to try to win that quarter. I think Cliff Keel, referred to as "Fuddy-Fup" in an earlier chapter on the 1953 football season won more quarters than anyone. Cliff went on to become a military and commercial pilot for many years so maybe the appeal to his competitive spirit in the ninth grade gave him the start to his later career. I never used the "quarter" trick when I was teaching, but I wasn't teaching math courses anyway. I did tell the "cook/killer" joke on more than one occasion however.

In 1991 I was living in Daytona Beach, Florida and met a lady who said she was from Nashville originally. As the conversation progressed it turned out she had gone to West High and graduated in 1942. I mentioned Doc and how much we all loved him so I was surprised to hear her say, "Oh we thought he was terrible." You can never expect unanimity, but I do think she was in the minority and most people shared the opinion expressed in Fred Russell's column.

There was a surprise visitor to the West locker room after the grueling game against Lake City. Kenneth Zink had been a Cavert Junior High teammate with Jimmy French in 1950 when a similar scenario had been played out. The 4'10" French had made a basket to tie the score against Waverly-Belmont in the closing seconds and Cavert went on to win the game. Zink was 6'3" at the time and it was believed they would continue as teammates at West End High School. However, Zink left school before his senior year and joined the Air Force. The afternoon paper displayed pictures side by side showing the two in 1950 in their basketball uniforms and in 1954 with French in a Blue Jay outfit, but Zink as an Airman. The difference in height was not as great in 1954 as it was four years earlier, but it was still obvious. There had been a lot of speculation before the season when it became known Zink would not be available to play center. However, the consistent play of Stephens and Gaines alternating at the position had made that a small worry as the final weekend approached.

Camera crews were at the school for the final Friday pep rally and you would think all activity at the school had stopped. In reality the games were a major focal point, but because of the late starting times many students had not attended the first two games. On Friday night the Blue Jays again had the 9:00 slot, but at least two people, me and Ralph Greenbaum, would have preferred an earlier time. We were both scheduled to be across town at 8:30 the next morning to take an all day college entrance exam which meant I had to pick him up about seven o'clock to make sure we got there on time. Plus in my case the high school golf season was starting and soon I would be playing in the two weekly matches. Most afternoons I was practicing at Richland, my home course, which was next to the high school, eating a quick supper, and heading to the games.

For a change West entered a game as a slight favorite (90.1 to 89.2) in the Litratings. At that time the Litratings were a sports barometer developed by a Vanderbilt engineering professor, Dr. E.E. Litkenhous, as a hobby. Today it is a national service which along with other ratings for many sports outgrew the good doctor's kitchen table years ago. Dr. Lit certainly indicated the game would be close and he was right, but it didn't start out that way.

The score was 12-4 at the end of the first quarter and all of Treadwell's points came on free throws. There was a little over three minutes left in the first half when the Eagles made their first field goal. With a lead of 24-14 at the half it looked like the "tired" West High team might actually have an easy game. But then things started happening and once again West was facing challenges that would take every bit of coaching knowledge Joe Shapiro had accumulated.

Treadwell got hot in the third quarter and pulled to within five points, 36-31. In that quarter Ralph Greenbaum got hit in the eye and had to leave the game. With 2:41 left to play Treadwell went ahead 38-37. This game was called more closely than the earlier ones and Eddie Gaines had fouled out in the first half. Butch Stephens picked up his fourth foul in the middle of the fourth quarter. Greenbaum, returning to play with a bandage above his right eye, also had four fouls. To add to the misery Jimmy French, who rarely fouled, had picked up his fourth as well. The injuries and large number of fouls made it necessary for Archie Grant, a rarely used substitute guard, to make a brief appearance in the game. With a minute and a half to play Jimmy French made a foul shot to tie the game and that's how it ended (38-38).

Treadwell's inability to finish their comeback, especially their failure to score in the last two and a half minutes, apparently took a toll on the players. They looked listless in the overtime as the one-eyed Greenbaum scored five points. French added another basket before fouling out and Butch Stephens made a foul shot. The final score was 46-40 and West was going to the finals for the first time since 1948. They had survived four overtime games in their nine game streak, all in the last seven, with a two point victory in there as well. But, this was a game that Treadwell would not have to look far to figure out how it was lost. They missed ten free throws in the regular game and six free throws in the overtime. West wasn't that much better, making 20 of 32, but it was enough.

WEST-LAFOLLETTE, MARCH 13

      Saturday morning started early for me at 3401 West End Avenue when I got into my parents car and made the short drive to the Greenbaum residence on Richardson Avenue. Right on time Ralph popped out of the house and the bandage over his eye was smaller and less noticeable than the night before. Ralph's version of the day's start is that he was escorted to the test by two female students, one of whom was a cheerleader which is certainly a more interesting story. Perhaps the fact that he had gone to the hospital after the game to have the cut over his eye stitched up properly affected his memory. Or maybe the passage of time has affected mine, but however we got there we both ended up in East Nashville and Isaac Litton High School for an all day schedule of College Board testing. With today's interstate highways the twelve mile journey would take less than a half hour. In 1954 it took close to an hour, even on a Saturday morning, taking West End to downtown, crossing the Cumberland River, and going out Gallatin Road with numerous traffic lights along the way.

We were among a small group of West End High School students taking the day long test. Today high school students start taking such tests before their senior years and the scores are a major factor in the admission process. In 1954 it was really only the Ivy League schools that required them, but since both Ralph and I aspired to go to Yale that's where we were on that Saturday morning. I felt fairly confident about the test because my brother had taken it two years earlier and was now a sophomore at Harvard. I had visited the Yale campus in 1948 with my father and fell in love with the place. He took me on a business trip which started in Washington, DC where I visited the Smithsonian. Then it was on to New York for a few plays and then the train ride from Grand Central Station to New Haven for the Vanderbilt-Yale football game. Vanderbilt won 35-0 as they moved toward a successful 8-2-1 season, but no bowl game. A family friend and West High graduate two years ahead of me was already a student at Yale and the possibility of Ralph going there as well made the dream that started in 1948 seem attractive. But, I knew I could go to Vanderbilt, which didn't require a College Board score, if the Yale application fell through.

Maybe I was talking to myself, but as I remember the drive Ralph and I hardly talked about the game the night before or the one coming up as we crawled through traffic. Actually we talked mostly about the upcoming test and strategies to take it. We had been told to try and answer the questions we knew and not spend too much time guessing at the ones we were not sure of. We were prepared for the prospect of not being able to answer all the questions in the allotted time because we were told most people didn't finish it completely. And so the morning began in a strange school building that was not that different from our own school. Similar to West End the Isaac Litton High School became a middle school a few years later. We felt good about the test and went to lunch at a Howard Johnson restaurant in the neighborhood. Greenbaum ate like a horse because this was the biggest meal he would have that day. We returned to take the afternoon test and when it was over it is fair to say we were both mentally exhausted. I let Greenbaum out at his house and went home in time to eat and then go watch the consolation game between Treadwell and Kingsport. Ralph and I were not the only students with a full agenda that day. Trumpeter and band leader John Kepler took first place in the music competition in Murfreesboro earlier in the day.

You might think the contest for third place would be a listless affair, but actually it was another exciting and close game like so many others in this tournament. Treadwell led at the half 28-23, but could not hold off Kingsport who roared back in the second half to win 53-51. It looked likely the Treadwell coach would spend a lot of time in the next season on free throw shooting. The team from Memphis could have been in the finals or at least taken home a third place trophy if they had been able to shoot fifty percent from the foul line.

With the consolation game over the crowd settled in for the championship contest and it appeared both the Treadwell fans and Kingsport supporters chose to sit in the west end zone of the gym joining the cheerleaders and fans for LaFollette. It is understandable that Treadwell would like to see the team that kept them from the finals lose. In the case of Kingsport I suppose it was just a case of geographical loyalty that made them support the lone East Tennessee team remaining in the tournament. There had been a rumor the night before that LaFollette was trying to recruit a band to partially offset the noise coming from the east end of the gym where the West fans were increasing in number every night. That would be a tall order because very few, if any, schools besides West had a band of any size at basketball games. In all probability they would have to find one in the Nashville area and the same geographical loyalty found in the East Tennessee schools would apply in Davidson County. Over the years I have had several conversations with people who went to Hillsboro, MBA, Father Ryan, and East. It is true they wanted to beat West when they played them, but there was no question who they were for in the 1954 state tournament.

Because there was no school the next day the Friday night semi finals had drawn the largest crowd of the tournament, 3,143. The finals on Saturday left that mark in the dust setting a state tournament record with a crowd of 4,034. For the week the total attendance was close to 14,000 and insured that Vanderbilt would get to host the tournament several times in future years.

One of the people who did not go to the games was Doc himself. The soon to be retired principal was diagnosed with heart problems and advised to stay away from the games because of the stress that might be produced. For several games he contented himself with following the games on the radio, but as the tournament progressed the emotional Munson broadcasts proved to be as hard on his nervous system as being there in person. For the final game he contented himself with receiving reports by telephone after each quarter from a friend.

LaFollette came into the tournament with an impressive 22-1 season record. Their only loss came at the hands of Knoxville East by two points. In January they beat Lake City 57-54 in an overtime game. These two teams from adjoining counties would meet three more times. LaFollette won the second regular season game and the district tournament final. They met again in the regional final and this time Lake City handed the Owls their second loss of the season. When they came to Nashville and were placed in different brackets it was not farfetched to think they might meet for the fifth time in a championship game. West shattered that dream matchup in overtime two nights earlier and now Lake City was back home and the Blue Jays had their sights set on a record fourth state championship. No one thought it would be easy and the Litratings showed the game as even: LaFollette (90.9); West (90.3). The big question marks were whether Greenbaum was going to be a factor, or had the eye injury and all day test taking session worn him out. His counterpart at guard French didn't take the day off, but was seen practicing foul shots in the West High gymnasium. The night before was a poor shooting night for both West and Memphis Treadwell and he did not want to see a repeat of that performance.

LaFollette was a taller team than West, but that was a familiar scenario. The Shapiro system on offense was based on making a pass and then following the ball to the man receiving it to set a screen. Both guards and the forwards, Billy Owens and Buddy Parsons, were disciplined to take short to medium range jump shots when they were available, but without a shot clock there was no need to fire away until you had an open shot. Gaines and Stephens at center played with their back to the basket and when they scored points it was usually a tip-in or a follow-up on a rebound. In most games the West centers matched up with the tallest player on the opposing team. It was at the other positions they gave away size so positioning (blocking out) was crucial for rebounding. On defense the Jays usually played a man-to-man defense and fought through screens rather than switching. That way the smaller guards rarely got caught trying to guard a much taller opponent and were in position to lead a fast break if there was a long rebound. No one would call West a high scoring fast breaking team, but when the opportunity presented itself they often outran the opposition for easy baskets. But, playing good team defense and keeping the game close was really their best weapon. It was obvious this team did not have an individual player who could dominate an opposing team the way Billy Joe Adcock did in 1946 or Bob Dudley Smith in 1948.

As the tipoff approached I was experiencing emotions similar to the last week of the football season. The realization that, win or lose, this journey was going to be over in a few hours was unsettling. It had been so much fun confounding the skeptics that a final victory might seem less enjoyable than the upsets and overtimes along the way. Obviously there was a curiosity about what kind of game the final one would turn out to be. Were we looking at overtime, sudden death, a cliffhanger, or a blowout like the Woodlawn game? My hunch was it would be another close one decided in the final minutes. I was right.

By now both papers were assigning multiple reporters to the game and photographers were taking pictures of the crowd, the cheerleaders, and anything else of interest. Edgar Allen referred to West as having an "800-person student body." Even if you counted the junior high grades the school wasn't that big, but there were probably close to 800 people crammed into the east end zone. Students, teachers, alumni, friends, and parents were all mixed together. Their goal for the game was to never sit down and never stop making noise. The pace of the game made that easy to achieve.

LaFollette led 14-11 at the end of the first quarter. They maintained their lead through a low scoring second quarter and led by six points at halftime (23-17). West was used to low scoring games, but they usually were nursing a lead in those contests. Greenbaum was noticeably tired and not scoring. Vaughn DuBose made an early appearance in the game, but he was the only substitute besides Gaines to see action. The good news was French and Buddy Parsons were taking up the slack and keeping the game fairly close. LaFollette wasn't playing a lot better and both teams were missing foul shots. Unlike the game the night before only Eddie Gaines was in foul trouble.

The third quarter started well for the Blue Jays. Buddy Parsons hit his first three shots as West went six for six from the field. Lafollette lost part of their halftime lead, but still lead by three points when the long journey entered its final eight minutes. Larry Munson was describing the West team, and especially their undersized guards, as if they were staggering survivors of the Bataan Death March in the Second World War. And then as if this was not enough drama a completely unforeseen event occurred. DOC CAME INTO THE GYM!

There are stories that abound of eye witness accounts of Babe Ruth "calling his shot" when he hit a home run at Wrigley Field in 1932 by people who weren't born at the time. It is said more people claim to have seen Bobby Thompson's home run at the Polo Grounds in 1951 than the capacity of the stadium. And so it is with the entrance of Dr. W.H. Yarbrough into the Vanderbilt Memorial Gymnasium at approximately 10:00 PM CST on March 13, 1954. Over the years I have heard a lot of different versions and while there are no major conflicts it is possible there are some embellishments. As one of the 4,034 in paid attendance I can only say what I remember. Actually when you count players, ushers, press, etc. there might have been 4,500 to 5,000 people there. I was so caught up in the game I didn't notice it at the time and later when I saw Doc was there I wondered "when did he get here?"

The story actually started a few hours earlier. Doc had made arrangements to learn of the progress of the game as each quarter came to an end. When he learned the team was behind by three points after one quarter he was concerned, but they had been down that road before. However, when he was told the deficit at halftime was six points and it had been as high as ten he decided "the boys need me." He called a friend to take him to the game and arrived there as the fourth quarter began so he could "console them."

The fourth quarter was a low scoring affair and the Owls increased their lead to four points midway through the period. With the score 39-35 West put on a defensive display that won the game. Lafollette failed to score the next time they had the ball. They fouled Butch Stephens who made both shots and now the score was 39-37. Lafollette couldn't score and then Buddy Parsons was fouled. His free throw made it 39-38 with less than two minutes to play. At that point it was assumed by most people in the stands that if West got the ball back they would run down the clock hoping for a foul or a chance for a last second shot to win.

To the amazement of everyone, and I include myself in this scenario, French drove toward the basket and threw up a running hook shot that went in! Now the score was West 40 LaFollette 39 with 1:37 to play. Hook shots are usually taken by taller players. For a five foot seven guard to even attempt one in a game is unheard of, and certainly not in a close game when you're behind. But, in addition to practicing foul shots earlier in the day French had also experimented with other off balance and unusual shots just in case he needed to make one that night. I might have missed Doc's entrance, but I had a good view of this shot and actually I had seen him take shots like that for three years. It was in all the way and now it was time to go back on defense. LaFollette took a quick shot which missed, but Chuck "Spider" Webb was fouled. He tied the game up after missing the first of two three throws (40-40). With the game now tied the West strategy was obvious. There would be no more off balance running hook shots. Jimmy French would dribble the ball and if he wasn't fouled in the final 57 seconds West would take the final shot. If it worked the Blue Jays had their fourth state championship. If not, the worst that could happen was another overtime game.

LaFollette wasn't buying it. They fouled French trying to steal the ball, but the guard who had suffered an eye injury in the first half only made one shot (41-40). Munson was enthralling listeners now with his narrative about the West guards only "having two eyes between them." People in the stands weren't sure what would happen next, but it was a repeat of the earlier scene. Webb missed a shot. French got the rebound. Webb fouled French. For the second time in less than a minute Jimmy French had a chance to either ice the game or insure an overtime period at the worst. Because there was no three point shot in 1954 if he made both foul shots the game would be out of reach. But, he missed the first one and made the second (42-40).

If there was ever a time for defense this was it. The West full court press kept the Owls from getting the ball over the center line. The ball turned over to the Blue Jays with nineteen seconds and another fine dribbling performance by French killed the clock. The crowd went wild. Players hugged each other. All City guard in football Gailor Justice was a meticulous scorekeeper for Coach Shapiro all year, but he could not contain himself and he scribbled "STATE CHAMPS" across the pages of the final game. Doc joined the team when the trophy was presented. They had indeed gone "All The Way For Doc."

As the crowd settled down after two hours of nonstop excitement and awaited the presentation of the trophies I saw a sight that has stuck with me to this day. The LaFollette players and cheerleaders, some crying, were consoling one another at the other end of the gym. My feelings at the time have not changed over the past years. They had nothing to feel bad about. They had played hard and lost a close game that could have gone either way. It is a scene I have watched play out over and over since then, and not always in an athletic contest. I have little patience with winners who gloat and having been on a few losing sides myself I think I understand how the LaFollette fans felt that night. One of my favorite newspaper pictures from that night is one where Doc is being hugged by a West cheerleader and Ralph Greenbaum. The fourth person in the picture offering his congratulations is LaFollette player Charles "Spider" Webb. The picture could just have easily been reversed. The game was that close.

THE CELEBRATION

On Sunday morning following the West victory the Tennessean sports pages covered the game as if there was no other news to report. The sports editor, Raymond Johnson, rarely mentioned high school sports, but this day he devoted his entire column to a state tournament he referred to as the "thrill-packed state tourney greatest in 30 year history." His recap of the three week march to victory by the Blue Jays contained nothing new of a factual nature, but his analysis of the team might have offended some fans. In tracing the history of the tournament which began in 1921 he said "the state tournament may have produced better teams than West's Blue Jays...There might have been better ones in this tournament." But, then he adopted the line which has become standard over the years by adding "...there has never been one with more spirit or fight than Joe Shapiro's boys displayed." In an interesting conclusion to his column Johnson's final paragraph was headed with the statement "Big Week of Basketball Thrilled Nashville Fans." He listed the five days and nights of the tournament along with the SEC playoff between Kentucky and LSU. He concluded with a mention of "the entertaining performance of the fabulous Globetrotters here yesterday afternoon." No mention was made of the upcoming National Negro High School tournament or the latest games played by the Nashville Business College team.

Jimmy Davy got to write the story of the game as well as a "High School Highlights" column with the headline "West's Mighty Midgets Rated Best Guards in NIL History." He didn't say who did the rating or what it was based on, but the consistent performance of the two short players was a major factor in the team's success all year, not just at tournament time. To call them "midgets" is a bit of a stretch. The term is defined as "a person of unusually small stature who is otherwise physically apportioned." The two boys were not unusually small (5'7" and 5'8") for the era in which they lived. Compared to the size of today's players the whole team would have to be considered short, not just French and Greenbaum. A few years later in 1966 the Kentucky Wildcats went to the finals of the NCAA tournament with a team nicknamed "Rupp's Runts." Averaging over six feet in height no more described those players as runts than the West guards as midgets. That UK team today is better known for the racial composition of the Texas Western (now Texas-El Paso) team that beat them in the finals 72-65. The all white Kentucky team lost to a team with eight minority players. It would be three more years before UK recruited their first African-American player, following Vanderbilt who had integrated the SEC three years earlier.

A third story was written by John Seigenthaler, the man who would later become the editor of the paper was a reporter at that time and not usually assigned to the sports section. His recap of the game was similar to Davy's and both men felt that the entrance of Doc in the second half was the turning point in the game. That's hard to argue with, but when you look at the missed free throws and turnovers by LaFollette in the final minutes it seems like the game was decided, like so many, by the team that made the fewest mistakes. Looking back at the previous three weeks West had several opportunities to lose games when the opposing team had the last shot. The overtime games of MBA, Donelson, Lake City, and Treadwell all left people on the losing side kicking themselves for missed opportunities.

Monday morning came and the Tennessean was still writing stories about the game and the team. Johnson again devoted his column to the week of basketball in the city. The final paragraph was also again about the performance of the Harlem Globetrotters who would probably return the following year for another "exhibition and marvelous halftime acts." Apparently he had no idea that Negro players had a desire to do anything other than serve as entertainment to a segregated audience.

The Banner got a chance to weigh in that afternoon for the first time since the afternoon paper did not have a Sunday edition. Their coverage had stories with now familiar headlines like "Determined Blue Jays Never Gave Up Hope." Another story said the "West End Miracle" all began on February 27th which was the night they beat MBA in a sudden death overtime game. Actually I believe it happened a few weeks earlier when the team made the drive back from East High after suffering their final loss of the season. At that point it would have been easy to assume this was a pretty good team on the way to a winning season and one that might win a few games in the tournament two weeks away. Certainly no one was saying out loud that this was a team that could add several more trophies to the already full cases in the front hallway of the school. That would have seemed like a miracle. Another news story had the accurate headline "Defense Pays Off For Jays." The statistics bore this out when it was shown their opponents averaged 41.25 points per game and West averaged 46. Their eight point victory over Petersburg was the only game they scored more than fifty points (51) in the state tournament. In all ten games in the three tournaments their opponents reached fifty only once when they beat Donelson 52-50 in the regional tournament.

For the next week the stories continued with much of the commentary consisting of a pat on the back to Vanderbilt for a well run tournament. There were accolades to the four officials who worked all sixteen games. Unlike today's use of three officials at that time there were only two officials per game which meant that for the first three days they had work two or three a day. Even without a shot clock the low scoring games still required a lot of running and the four officials actually put in more time on the court than any of the teams. Edgar Allen found room to praise Oakley Christian, West High's football captain and basketball manager, for his quick retrieval of a loose ball in the Lake City game when it not only went out of bounds, but into the seated area beside the unusually wide court. The Banner even put the victory on the editorial page with a cartoon by political cartoonist Jack Knox. Knox drew a striking likeness of both Doc and the clock tower of the school, but that came as no surprise. He had two sons who were West graduates and former football players. His daughter was a junior in the school at the time of the tournament. In the cartoon Doc is shown receiving a ball which says "The Champ 1954". It is said to be from "his kids who wouldn't quit!!" The bruised and bedraggled player in the drawing hardly looks like the smiling players in the photos receiving the trophy, but the words are probably more appropriate than those of the sports reporters. The team ended up with their fourth state trophy simply because they overcame a lot of obstacles to victory and outlasted the other teams.

The trophies were not placed in a trophy case immediately in part because there really was not enough room in the already crowded fixtures in the school entrance hallway. So for the week following the final victory they just sat on the counter in the school office for all to see up close and even touch them if they chose. Sometime following the close of school on Thursday, March 18th the trophies were not just looked at and touched…they were stolen! The motivation for the theft was hard to figure because the large items had no value at a pawn shop because they were obviously the property of the school whose name was inscribed on them. There had been a wave of youthful vandalism in Nashville at that time, but the brazen taking of items from inside a building did not fit into the pattern of other incidents. It was probably just a prank by someone who was making a statement. It could have been a West High student who was unhappy with the attention the team was receiving or it might be someone from an opposing school who was unhappy at being defeated by the Bluejays in the tournament. Whatever it was it did not change the outcome of the tournament. It was just a nuisance to put up with.

It certainly put a damper on the two festivities scheduled for Friday, March 19th when the team was honored at both a luncheon and a dinner. At noon they were the guests of the Optimist Club and that evening there was a dinner at Richland Country Club. In addition to the team and coaches, former players George Kelley,

Billy Joe Adcock, and Bob Dudley Smith were invited. This was a long time before players expected individual rings in celebration of a championship, but they did each receive a small pen knife (which would keep you from boarding a plane today) that said "State Basketball Champions 1954." The dinner was paid for by my father so I got to attend, but I didn't get a knife. At a class reunion in 1998 Coach Shapiro mentioned the dinner and the presents Dad had donated. To my amazement there were at least three people in the room who still had the small pen knifes on their key rings that day.

The following week the plot thickened when two prank calls were made to Coach Shapiro, one asking for money in exchange for the return of the trophies and the other saying the items were on the front steps of the school. Actually the trophies were found in a wooded area next to the school a short time later and a reward of $100 was divided among the three young children who discovered them. It was obvious the items had been taken somewhere else immediately after the theft because the area where they were found had been thoroughly searched several times. They were covered with some foliage, but obviously had not been exposed to the weather for a ten day period. The only damage was a small basketball broken off of the District tournament trophy.

At the all sports banquet following the return of the trophies Dr. Yarbrough showed no bitterness and simply quipped that the perpetrators had given the team "two weeks of additional publicity." Also at that dinner Doc said he had received a communication from rival coach Howard Allen. Allen had been the coach at MBA for many of the years that West failed to beat them in football. He left MBA to coach a short time in Texas and then returned to Nashville where he coached at Father Ryan. When West beat Ryan in football earlier in the year it was described as the first time they had ever beaten a team coached by Howard Allen. I had known Allen a few years earlier when he was one of the owners of Camp Mountain Lake, a summer camp my brother and I went to for several summers. Allen sold his interest in the camp after one year which many felt had simply been a way for him to keep an eye on his MBA players during the summer. There certainly were a number of them, as well as junior high prospects, there as campers or counselors. My recollection was that Allen spent a lot of time fishing in the artificial lake and he did seem to catch a lot of fish.

What Allen had said about the West High players was that he was going to write down the names of these ten young men and check in ten years to see how they were doing. He was convinced they would all be successful if they continued to show the courage and determination they had displayed in winning the tournament.

While the West High victories got most of the coverage during the month of March 1954, they were not the only games in town. On Thursday, March 25th the National Negro High School tournament began at Tennessee A & I. Teams from Florida, Oklahoma, Virginia, Illinois, Kentucky, Mississippi, Georgia, Louisiana, Alabama, North Carolina, Arkansas, joined two teams from Tennessee (Clarksville and Knoxville) for three days of basketball. Both papers covered the games in a matter of fact manner. There were no box scores, or stories about individual players, although undoubtedly there were several participants that college recruiters (outside the South) were interested in.

Earlier that week the Nashville Business College women's team advanced in the AAU tournament in St. Joseph, Missouri before losing to Wayland College of Plainview, Texas 38-21. The coverage of AAU women's basketball was not that different from the stories about the national Negro tournament. The only embellishment was the inclusion of box scores for the NBC games.

Back at West High the baseball team started practice with six basketball players (French, Greenbaum, Grant, Glenn, DuBose, and Parsons) and two managers (Christian and Lewis) from the state championship team looking to avenge the near miss at a championship trophy from the previous year. Because of the large number of returning starters and the addition of several talented newcomers West was a favorite to repeat as district champion.

I prepared for my final year as member of the West High golf team, the sixth straight year a member of my family had been on the team. Unfortunately there were several teams loaded with good players, particularly Ryan and East, and although I had a good year with an average nine hole score of 39, it wasn't good enough to get me in the individual tournament at the end of the season. A bad round of 44 in the rain against Doc Tant of East knocked me out of the top eight players who made the tournament. Another low point of the year was when I shot a two over par 38 and was beaten decisively by Louie Graham who birdied four of the first six holes. The only other loss was to Bobby Calton of MBA.

The baseball team looked like they would duplicate, if not exceed, the record of the previous year. Unfortunately after an undefeated regular season they were eliminated by Tullahoma in the Midstate tournament for their only loss of the season. Second baseman Jimmy French and pitcher Jimmy Lewis made the All-Nashville team. Ralph Greenbaum made the Western Division team as well. It was a complex year for Ralph who started the year in centerfield and then moved to the unfamiliar position of catcher. However, his hitting didn't suffer with the change of positions and that is what gave him the most recognition. By his own admission he was no more than adequate at the new position. Shortstop Archie Grant and left handed pitcher Skippy Kelly also got honorable mention, but a case could be made for Vaughn DuBose as well. The outfielder also served as the Jays third pitcher and had two clutch wins in the league championship series. For the year it gave West an impressive record of 50 wins, 7 losses, and 1 tie in the three major sports. It is hard to find reliable statistics on the topic, but it is possible that three sport record is the best any school in Nashville ever achieved up to that time.

Even though his time as a high school principal was coming to an end Doc was not through with public life. He decided to run for the city council in the West End district because of his dislike for the political machine that dominated elections in the area at that time. Many former students lived in the district and campaigned for their former principal. His popularity made him an easy winner and he served from 1955 to 1959, but he had little success in convincing the council to change their ways. The heart problem that kept him from attending basketball games was not improved by the rigors of the political arena. He died on June 25, 1961.

It is tempting to speculate about how well Doc would have coped with the changes that took place at West End after his retirement. However, there are several reasons to believe he would have handled the change from a segregated high school to an integrated middle school quite well. He had spent several years before coming to West as principal at the Peabody Demonstration School which had grades from Kindergarten to the 12th grade in the same building. All his years at West were spent as principal of grades 7-12, so he had plenty of experience dealing with students of all ages.

There is also reason to believe that Dr. W.H. Yarbrough would have not been fazed by the efforts to comply with the requirements of Brown vs. the Board of Education. In 1932 his doctoral dissertation was published entitled "Economic Aspects Of Slavery In Relation To Southern and Southwestern Migration." This scholarly examination of an explosive topic is well thought out and expressed in an objective fashion. It is neither the romantic defense of the South nor the harsh condemnation of the region that other authors were writing in the first half of the 20th century. It is just my opinion, but I think it gives the impression that Doc would have dealt with the legal challenges to the status quo in an even handed manner. While he may have appeared to be the personification of the "absent-minded professor," he was unwavering in his dedication to the education of students. A close reading of his dissertation indicates that in 1932 he was probably not going to be surprised, or upset, at the 1954 Supreme Court ruling.

THE INTERVENING YEARS

I don't know if Howard Allen was right in his prediction or if he even followed up on it in later years. Ralph Greenbaum did become a doctor, and while he was the only person on the basketball team to do that he wasn't the only person in the class who went to medical school. As far as I know none of the ten players (eleven if you count Jerry Morrison) turned out badly and the ones I am aware of did quite well.

With the perspective of hindsight it appears that the West High "miracle" was the beginning of the last gasp of the life we knew as teenagers. Life in Nashville today bears almost no resemblance to what life was like in the 1950s. Some of the changes are obvious and were predictable. Others are like the bursting of a dike and where the water goes after that is anybody's guess. If there is a single event that represents the moment the changes began it would have to be the Supreme Court decision outlawing segregation in public schools. When news of the court's ruling reached Nashville it was obvious changes would have to be made, but no one was predicting what the changes would be, or when they would occur.

In many ways the decision seemed to catch Nashville by surprise and certainly unprepared. In doing the research for this book I discovered there was no justification for the surprise. There were news stories about the pending Brown vs. The Board of Education case for several years leading up to May of 1954 and a great deal of speculation about what the court's ruling would be. It could just as easily have been a Tennessee case because there were several joined together including the one from Clinton, Tennessee. The plaintiff Brown just happened to come first alphabetically. Even though the concept of "separate, but equal" had been upheld earlier in the century it was obvious that concept was being erased in a step by step fashion. The Board of Education referred to in the Brown case was in Topeka, Kansas. While it was generally thought then and now that the practice of segregation was a Deep South issue, it is obvious this was untrue. Kansas was certainly not a state anyone ever associated with the Old Confederacy.

The expense of maintaining separate school systems had been extremely burdensome on southern communities during the Depression and Second World War. And the reality was it was impossible to actually maintain truly separate systems in an equal fashion. It was possible to make an attempt at the grammar school level, but as minority children got older and wanted to attend high school, college, and graduate school it got complicated. Plus it was terribly unfair. If a Negro student in Anderson County, Tennessee wanted to attend high school they had to make a forty mile bus trip to a segregated high school in Knoxville. Minority students in Davidson County, Tennessee all attended the one high school for Negroes in the unincorporated area surrounding Nashville, a distance of anywhere from five to fifty miles. Within the city limits there were three colored schools as well as six for whites. Often there would two schools within a mile of one another admitting different races. Howard (white) was a short distance across Lafayette Street from Cameron (black). Meigs (black) was several blocks down Main Street from East (white). From my home the route we drove to North (white) for games took us right by Pearl (black). Because of the dual government, city and county, before merger in the 1960s there were in effect four different systems.

The difference in per pupil expenditures and teacher salaries had been the subject of several lawsuits in Nashville long before the Brown decision. The plaintiffs were successful in practically all the cases, but even with physical improvements to the black schools it was obvious they were not equal. For many years Pearl was the only black high school in Nashville, but the demand for education was so great that two other schools, Meigs and Cameron were added. Even with the expansion the minority schools still had enrollments and class size greater than any of the white schools. After the Brown decision there were some improvements made to the schools in a hasty effort to show that the concept of "separate, but equal" was being met. Cynics would say with justification that Meigs was improved to avoid integration at East Nashville High School because Meigs was the only black high school in the city on the east side of the river. Although the black teachers association had won an equal pay lawsuit their average pay was less than the earnings of white teachers because of a complex system of evaluating teachers.

If a black student wanted to go to college they had a choice of one public institution, Tennessee A&I in Nashville. There were a number of private colleges in Tennessee, including Fisk in Nashville. But, the opportunities for graduate study were very limited at these schools. This had led to a lawsuit which integrated the graduate programs at the University of Tennessee in Knoxville several years before the Brown decision.

It is hard to understand why students of my generation did not see what was coming, but I suppose we were just too caught up in our own little worlds to see the obvious. It was certainly an underreported subject and the two newspapers were not much help. The afternoon Banner was staunchly segregationist and believed any attempts to alter the "Southern way of life" had to be communist inspired. While the morning Tennessean was far more liberal in most matters than the Banner they were hardly leaders in the charge for social change. Their stance was moderate at best and tended to favor peaceful integration from the perspective of law and order rather than any kind of moral imperative. As the 1950s moved into the 1960s the number of television stations grew from one to three and the opportunities to show pictures expanded greatly. Sometimes it was a peaceful demonstration and other times it was an out of control riot, but it was obviously a subject no one could ignore any longer.

After the Brown decision in 1954 Nashville governments and schools grappled with the question of how to proceed. The choices ranged between staunch resistance and refusal to comply or the immediate merger and integration of all the school systems. The gap between the two positions probably contributed to the virtual inaction on the subject for the next ten years. My father had publicly endorsed compliance with the decision in an orderly manner. He was the first president of a new organization, The Tennessee Human Relations Council, which tried to serve as a mediating force in the controversy. His efforts and those of others while noble had little effect on the outcome. It would take the orders of the United States District Court and the merger of the city and county governments to achieve any meaningful compliance. The Federal Court had approved an initial plan in the late 1950s, but it was so weak that it achieved almost no integration of the grammar schools affected.

My family had always been liberal when it came to matters of race. My uncle Jordan Stokes had been a lawyer for the NAACP in the 1940s in a lawsuit brought on behalf of Negro firemen. He also was the lawyer for the Highlander Folk School near Monteagle, Tennessee which sponsored integrated workshops dealing with labor organization and civil rights. Both Rosa Parks and Martin Luther King, Jr., attended integrated workshops there years before they became well known. My family's liberalism did not interfere with my social life as a student and fraternity member at Vanderbilt between 1954 and 1958, but it was obvious to me that my views on race were not in step with most of my classmates. My father was appointed to the Board of Trustees of Fisk University, but died shortly after his appointment in 1957. He had clashed on more than one occasion with Vanderbilt English professor Donald Davidson who was one of my instructors in college. I never had any reason to believe that Dr. Davidson brought his views into the classroom and certainly did not detect any bias toward me for whatever views I might have. Actually what views I did have on the subject were largely kept to myself. Vanderbilt in the 1950s was not a hotbed of political activity. This would change dramatically in the 1960s, but by then I was a practicing attorney in Nashville and free to get even more actively involved in civil rights than my uncle and father had ever been.

Changes were occurring at West End High School even before school integration and governmental merger dictated wholesale changes. The little gymnasium above the cafeteria remained, but a separate structure was built next to the school in the wooded area where the stolen trophies had been found a few years earlier. It was appropriately named the W.H. Yarbrough Gymnasium. Coach Shapiro was replaced as football coach by Jim Kennedy, but he continued to coach basketball and baseball. He had some good teams, but never again reached the heights of the championship teams of Emmet Strickland or his 1954 squad. However his teams were competitive and did come close to duplicating those feats a few times.

Certainly there were high hopes for the1954-1955 team following the state champions which had seven returning players. But after a fast start the team struggled late in the season. On February 15th they were upset by Peabody 29-43. The victory was a sweet one for the Tigers who had five players who had suffered four one sided losses to the Blue Jays the two previous years. Eddie Gaines who had been a big part of the team the year before saw his playing time reduced and quit the team in mid season. In a rare move Coach Shapiro dressed a ninth grader, Ronnie Sharer, for the remainder of the season after the junior high season ended. A first round loss to Father Ryan in the District Tournament ended the season for the defending state champs.

The 1955-1956 group could have been named the "younger brother" team with Charlie Greer, Wendell Stephens, and Bob Morrison trying to recapture the "All The Way For Doc" spirit older brothers Eddie, Butch, and Jerry had been a part of. In 1963, 1964, and 1965 Robert Greer played for West as the only "three brother" letter winners I am aware of. There are a lot of pairs of brothers, but this was the only trio I know of. This pales by comparison to Father Ryan which has numerous families that have sent as many as four and five sons to play for the Irish.

There were high hopes in 1956 when they had a winning season and won the 18th District Tournament, but lost to Isaac Litton in the Regional. The following year, 1956-1957 was a repeat performance with a District victory and a loss in the Regional to Bellevue. By then Ronnie Sharer was a senior and the dominant player on the high school scene. An upset loss to Hume-Fogg in the District Tournament put an abrupt end to the Jays' hopes for a fifth state crown. Sharer went on to play on the freshman team at Vanderbilt and then transferred to Belmont.

By that time I had become more engrossed in college basketball as a Vanderbilt student and rarely attended a high school game. West did make two more trips to the State tournament in 1959 and 1960. The 1959 team was something of a surprise, but after a winning season they rolled through the District beating Mt. Juliet, Peabody, and Cohn. Then they beat Waverly, DuPont, and Litton to return to the State Tournament for the first time since the All The Way For Doc team. The bubble burst in the first game when Memphis Treadwell pulled out a two point victory 45-47. It was revenge of sorts for Treadwell who lost in overtime to the Blue Jays in a semifinal game in 1954.

The 1959-1960 team made it back to the State Tournament, but it took an unorthodox path. Their regular season record was impressive and made them one of the seeded teams in the District Tournament. They easily beat Cohn in their first game 63-41. But, then they lost to Hume-Fogg 47-49. Ordinarily this would have been the end, but because of the expansion of the State Tournament three teams would advance from the 18th District making the usually meaningless consolation game very important. West beat Lipscomb and moved on to the Regional where they beat Erin in the first game.

They got revenge in the rematch with Hume-Fogg and victories over Gallatin and Dover put Joe Shapiro back in the State Tournament for the third time in seven years. Their first game was against LaFollette, the team they beat for the title in 1954. The players in this game were probably in the fifth or sixth grade at that time so any historical significance of the rematch was undoubtedly lost on them. West won 53-41 in a game that was actually close for the first three quarters. Following a 49-39 win over Sparta, West's hopes for a fifth title were dashed by Union City 50-55 and a 41-73 loss to Murfreesboro in the consolation game ended the saga of West high basketball in the state tournament. But in a sixteen year period (1944-1960) two coaches, Strickland and Shapiro, had gone to the tournament eight times filling up the trophy cases in the front hallway of the school.

As the decade of the 60s began the West High schedule changed and new county schools like Glencliff, Hillwood, Stratford, and Overton began to appear on the schedule, but that was far from the only change. Integration and the imitation of a UCLA style full court press made Father Ryan more than the Blue Jays could handle at a game I did attend in 1964. Willie Brown was the first black player for a Nashville high school and his leaping ability was impressive. The pressing defense with familiar names like Lynch, Mondelli, and Clunan was too much for the coach's wife. When Oakley Christian and I talked with Ruth Shapiro after the game she was practically in tears saying that type of defense "should be illegal."

West was facing more than new schools in the Metro school system which had replaced the old segregated systems when government was divided between city and county. Now the Bluejays were playing teams from the former "colored" system. In 1966 they lost in the Regional to Cameron 38-39. The following year they lost to Pearl (36-46) in the District tournament. But, the ten point loss was an improvement over Pearl's one sided victory (31-53) in the regular season.

When the 1967-68 season began there were no expectations for the team which had no veteran players. But, the greater uncertainty was the future of the school which was being phased out as a high school. It was a rare losing season for Joe Shapiro and when the 18th District tournament opened they were underdogs to familiar rival Cohn. It was only fitting that the games were being played at the "new" West High gym which was built after all the

State titles had been won. With a flair for the dramatic West won a triple overtime game 51-49. Two nights later the curtain fell on West End high school basketball when North beat the Blue Jays 38-59. Joe Shapiro's head coaching career was over with a record of 360 wins and 156 losses in all sports at five different schools. It is certainly an "apples and oranges" comparison, but Cornelius Ridley, the long time Pearl High coach, had a career record of 684-171. Even more astounding is the 689-94record of John Head at the Nashville Business College. However, if you combine the records of the two coaches at West End High School, Strickland (151-20) and Shapiro, the win total approaches those of Ridley and Head. Also, Shapiro's last years at the school were some of his biggest losers as the transition from high school to middle school began to occur. Any way you look at it there was some excellent coaching in the Nashville area during the 1940s, 50s, and 60s regardless of the sex or race of the players. However Joe Shapiro's coaching days were not over after retiring from the school system he coached the basketball team at MBA from 1976-1979.

It is also fitting that Jimmy Davy got to write the story of the last game for the Tennessean and Edgar Allen covered the game for the Banner, but I didn't notice that until I did the research for this book. I am sorry to say I was hardly aware of what was happening at and to my former school during its last days. 1968 was an incredible year in American history with the decision of President Johnson to not run for reelection and the assassinations of Martin Luther King and Robert Kennedy. Nashville was under a curfew part of that time because of riots in North Nashville. The murder of two policemen in January occupied a lot of my time when I was hired to defend one of the men accused of the crime. If anything was happening in high school basketball at that time I'm afraid I was too busy to notice it. Ironically the murder case involved a policeman, Wayne Thomason, who had gone to West a few years after me, but he was not someone I knew well. I discovered later that year that the court reporter who transcribed the lengthy trial was the sister of Banner sportswriter Edgar Allen. Nashville really was a much smaller town back then.

I am not familiar with what happened to many of the players who were part of the West High teams other than 1954. I know most of the players on that team did go on to college and while four of them played basketball none had the success they enjoyed in high school. Jimmy French went to Vanderbilt where he played basketball. The guard who was thought to be too short to play in the SEC was primarily a substitute until his senior year when he started several games. Ralph Greenbaum went to Yale for two years and then transferred to Vanderbilt where he played both basketball and baseball. He rarely played for the basketball team, but he is in the record book in baseball, getting six hits in one game against Middle Tennessee State (now MTSU). Archie Grant was a rarely used guard on the West High basketball team, but his skills as a baseball player earned him several college letters in that sport for the Commodores. Jimmy Lewis was a manager on the basketball team and spent four years as a pitcher/outfielder for the Vanderbilt baseball team. Billy Owens played basketball at Birmingham Southern for one year before transferring to Belmont where he joined another West High player, Eddie Greer. Greer was the only player to have a basketball career beyond college, but that was as a high school coach and not a player. Jimmy French also coached the Vanderbilt freshman team his last year in school having completed his four years of eligibility. Certainly none of the former Blue Jays had a college athletic experience that was near their high school experience, but they all received an education which was probably what Howard Allen had been talking about in 1954 anyway.

When I started writing this book I knew that West had undergone a dramatic change as a school, but I did not realize their story was not unique. In order to meet legal requirements and accommodate shifts in population the Davidson County school system of today is completely different from the one I knew as a teenager. There are eighteen public high schools today and very few of them were in existence when I graduated. Two that existed in the 1950s, East High and Hume-Fogg, have changed their mission. The downtown school, Hume-Fogg, used to be a vocational school and is now an academic magnet, and one of the most outstanding schools in the nation. East High is a magnet for literature and draws students from all over the county, not just the area on the east bank of the Cumberland River. Only Hillsboro is similar to the school I once knew. But, back then I regarded Hillsboro as a suburban school. Today people call it "inner-city," although I think the busing of students has more to do with that description than the location of the building.

Many of the buildings have ceased to be schools, but now house various academic programs. Cavert Junior High, Waverly-Belmont Junior High, Central High School, and Cohn High School all fall into that category. Howard High School is a government office building and North High does not exist in any fashion. A new school with a different name, John Early Middle School, was erected at the location where the Yankees once played. The toll on black schools was equally devastating. Haynes disappeared completely as a high school and became a middle school in a new building. Meigs and Cameron kept their buildings, but became middle schools like West End. The building that housed Pearl High is now Martin Luther King Middle School. The new and larger high school in the North Nashville area is named Pearl-Cohn, a curious mixture of two names from opposite sides of the segregated era.

The private schools tell a similar story. Father Ryan admitted girls after merging with Cathedral and moved to a larger campus in the suburbs. Only MBA remains in the same location, but there are new buildings and athletic fields crammed into every inch of space at their West End Avenue location. The big growth has been in private schools and academies which sprang up in many cases as a reaction to integration. The larger private schools now have their own separate football conference comprised of schools in Nashville, as well as others in Chattanooga and Memphis.

The remaining schools play in various classifications based on size and there is a month long playoff system to determine the different schools that can claim to be state champions. It is a far cry from the simple nine game schedule West played in 1953 which ended with a winning record (6-2-1) and no more games to play.

Integration and expansion made for changes in basketball as well. The National Negro High School Basketball tournament survived until 1967, but the integration of schools in the south led to its demise. However, before it was cancelled Pearl High had participated in the tournament seventeen times and won four championships (1958, 1959, 1960, and 1963). Next the Tigers set their sights on the Tennessee high school championship which they won three times (1965, 1966, and 1981). The first year they were allowed to play in the tournament was 1965 and the games were held at Vanderbilt gymnasium. One of the outstanding players on the Pearl team was Perry Wallace, who went on to play at Vanderbilt. Wallace, who is a charter member of the Vanderbilt Athletic Hall of Fame, was the first black basketball player in the SEC. Wallace was more than an athlete and he used his engineering degree to attend law school at Columbia and has been a professor at American University in Washington, DC for many years. Integration did not hurt ticket sales at the school, but created a need to build additional balconies on the south side of the gym to accommodate the crowds. When West won their fourth championship trophy before a half full gym no one would have predicted that within a little more than a decade later an all black team would win the trophy before a crowd twice the size of the one in 1954.

The state tournament of today bears no resemblance to the ones won by West End High or Pearl when all schools could play and there was one champion. Just like football there are now various classifications and more than one winner. The days when a small school like Woodlawn or Linden with less than 100 students could take home the one trophy that said state champs are gone forever. But, so are the days when boys played multiple sports and dreams, perhaps fantasies, of a college scholarship or a pro career were unheard of. Maybe some of the better athletes thought about a college athletic scholarship, but professional sports were almost unheard of in my youth. I didn't know anything about the National Basketball Association (NBA) until my brother went away to Harvard and talked about the Boston Celtics when he came home. Before that I just knew there was a team in Minneapolis, Minnesota, a state which claimed to have 10,000 lakes, called the Lakers and they had a tall player named George Mikan. They moved to Los Angeles and kept the nickname although LA has almost no lakes. But, the Jazz moved from New Orleans where the name made sense and went to Salt Lake City so I don't suppose it is necessary for a team to have a nickname that matches their location. Los Angeles has more examples than the Lakers. The Brooklyn Dodgers were actually called Trolleydodgers because of the tracks one had to cross to get into Ebbetts Field. Today the trolleys are gone, Ebbetts Field is a housing project, and the Dodgers play in an area of Los Angeles that can only be reached by automobile.

In my youth pro football was even more obscure. Television was available on a regional basis and all we got was the Washington Redskins because they were the southernmost team. Cynics say we actually got to watch them because the owner George Preston Marshall refused to sign Negro players. All I knew was they played in dark Griffith Stadium and the games looked even darker on a black and white TV. The team was always losing and the games were no fun to watch. The only local professional athletes I heard of were the one or two high school baseball players who got tryouts with major league teams and went to the minors. The days of signing bonuses and million dollar salaries were in the far distant future. Even players who were in the major leagues supplemented their incomes with off season jobs.

There were major rule changes in basketball that make the game of today a far cry from the brand played by the Blue Jays in the 1940s and 50s. The shot clock and three point shot puts a greater emphasis on offense than a Strickland or Shapiro team would have ever practiced. But, it wasn't just the game that changed. It is the color and sex of the players as well. It took a little longer for women to find a role in high school and college sports than it took to integrate the men's sports. During that time the AAU teams had their greatest years, but their days were numbered. The NBC teams of the 1940s coached by Leo Long and starring players like Aileen Banks were successful, but nothing like the later teams coached by John Head and led by Nera White. It was just a matter of time before the Vanderbilt gym would attract more fans to watch a women's game than saw the West High Blue Jays win a state championship. And the annual Vanderbilt-UT game draws more fans than ever saw any game when I was in school. Of course over half of them are wearing orange.

There was a predictable growth in girls' basketball at the high school level in the decades after West won its last state championship. There were very few schools in the county that played the game before the 1960s and West was never one of them. Ironically Coach Shapiro's daughter Laura attended Hillsboro rather than West so she could play basketball. This was a case of history repeating itself because her mother had played guard for Riverton High School in Alabama years earlier. Although there were District and Regional tournaments there was no State girls' tournament until 1958. The game was played with six on a side until 1980 when the present game of five on five was adopted. The record of four championships by West pales by comparison to the Shelbyville Eaglettes who won it twelve times, two with six starters (1964 and 1974) and ten times with five (1986, 1989, 1990, 1991, 1992, 1995, 2000, 2001, 2003, and 2004). Gene Pearce, who wrote the book about Linden basketball, Boys In Black, also wrote a book about the incredible success of the Shelbyville girl's team, Only Eaglettes Understand. It is similar to the tone of the books cited earlier about small town basketball in Illinois, Indiana, and Kentucky. The outside world knows Shelbyville, Tennessee for the Tennessee Walking Horse Show, but girls' basketball is the hot topic locally from November to March in Bedford County.

Sports were not the only thing that underwent change in the last half of the century. When I was a senior in college Nashville was in the process of building its first truly tall building. Today the L&C Tower is dwarfed by several taller buildings in the downtown area. L&C stood for the Life and Casualty Insurance Company which at one time was one of the largest insurers in the country. Another local company, National Life & Accident Insurance was even larger and in the 1960s built a taller building. Today both companies are gone and the buildings are leased to various government offices.

Insurance wasn't the only casualty of the late 20th century. The locally owned major banks built tall buildings as well only to see them acquired by larger regional banks. The two newspapers were reduced to one when the Banner went the way of afternoon papers all across the country. The downtown department stores fled to suburban malls and the city became a ghost town after dark. Even the Grand Ole Opry left the Ryman Auditorium for an Opryland theme park in the suburbs.

But, the emerging music industry needed an entertainment outlet and as night clubs began to fill in the abandoned areas of downtown the central city underwent a revival. But, if you want to shop or see a movie you're out of luck. Professional sports, hockey and football, added new arenas and big crowds. The airport expanded while passenger train service ceased and Union Station became an eyesore and then a hotel. Interstate highways made travel around the city much quicker and the metropolitan area grew to include several surrounding counties. As the end of the twentieth century approached the "Athens of the South" had become "Music City, USA."

REUNION

As 2004 approached it was inevitable people would be thinking about the 50 year anniversary of the "All The Way For Doc" team. But, as several of my classmates and I began meeting and planning it was obvious that we wanted the event to be more than a celebration about what a few boys in short pants had done five decades earlier. There were only five members of that team who graduated in 1954 and two of them, Billy Owens and Jerry Morrison, were too ill to attend the reunion. Because I had some computer skills the task of preparing a data base and web site fell in my lap. Actually it was guided into my lap by me because I felt it would be necessary to utilize the internet if we were going to have a first rate event.

As I began the effort I was fortunate to receive an almost up to date mailing list of the class of 1954. There had been a few attempts at reunions for the entire school in the 1990s which resulted in various class rosters being compiled. There were 151 names on our class list, 70 male and 81 female. On that list there were 14 with no address and an additional 28 classmates were known to be deceased. So we were beginning with a potential list of 109 people and they were scattered geographically. There were 67 with a Tennessee address and most of them were either in Nashville or an adjoining county. Florida was next with seven. Texas, Virginia, and California had three classmates. There were nine states with two and eight with a single member. There were no addresses outside the United States, but there was one in Hawaii. An initial mailing and questionnaire went out to the people on the list which generated a good response, but there were an additional 34 people who either never responded or for whom the address was bad. The general response of the remaining 75 indicated most people favored an event of more than one day and at least one of the events should be held at the school. There was little interest in having anything formal, although one person did specify "tuxedo and formal wear" for the Friday dinner. Later mailings included an appeal for contributions as well as payment for the scheduled events.

A year before the reunion would be held it was obvious the total bill was going to be more than the cost of the various meals. In order to have the necessary seed money a number of people agreed to put up deposits and in some cases pay for different parts of the event and the final schedule was set. A dinner was scheduled at Hillwood Country Club on Friday, June 18th and Larry Munson agreed to attend and be the main speaker. Munson had been a young man when he thrilled audiences with his broadcasts of minor league baseball and high school sports in Nashville. He moved up to Vanderbilt football and basketball and when major league baseball came to the south he moved to Atlanta as one of the announcers for the Braves. That did not last very long, but Munson moved on to the University of Georgia games and was the play-by-play man there until his retirement in 2008. The eclectic Munson also did TV shows on fishing as well as a radio jazz broadcast in addition to sports for many years commuting between Nashville, Atlanta, and Athens, Georgia.

We received permission to use the school cafeteria for a box lunch and the auditorium for a memorial ceremony for deceased classmates on Saturday. However, we were restricted from an unlimited tour of the school because of the construction taking place. Little did we know that was a remodeling project that would last for the next four years and prevent several classes following ours from having access to the building for their reunions. An informal cookout final event for Saturday night was scheduled at the Legends Golf Club near Franklin, Tennessee. The club is the home course for the Vanderbilt golf teams and I played in a scramble there in 2003. I was familiar with all the facilities we would be using and felt comfortable about the itinerary. So the schedule was set and the invitations went out.

There were fifty four classmates who came to the dinner on Friday night, but the addition of spouses and invited guests brought the total to almost one hundred. The majority of attendees were from the Nashville area, but twenty one graduates from out of state made the trip. If a prize was given to the person traveling the longest distance it would go to Cecelia Linam Fordham from Hawaii.

The website had been in place for over a year and email had replaced regular mail as the primary means of communication for many people. The website contained historical information about the school and Doc, as well as a summary of the athletic achievements of our senior year. It also served as a source of information about people who had submitted biographical information. Unfortunately it also contained a lot of obituary news as well. When the website appeared on the internet it confused a lot of people outside our class who believed it was a source of information about the entire school history instead of just one class. Some people even suggested it should be expanded beyond the narrow scope of 1954, but I wasn't interested in being that generous with my time. Having served its original purpose the website (classof54.com) was discontinued in 2009.

There was also a printed program for the affair, name tags were printed, and a commemorative lapel pin prepared. It appeared everything was set for an eventful weekend. What could go wrong? Not much, but there were a number of minor glitches that are more humorous than harmful in retrospect. I got to Hillwood a little early on Friday night and everything seemed to be ready except the name tags had not arrived yet. As more and more people came in the door it was getting increasingly awkward by the minute to pretend to recognize people who had in many cases gained weight, lost hair, or both since the last time you saw them. Certainly no one had lost weight, but a number of people looked enough like their yearbook picture (with gray hair) to provide for remarks like "you haven't changed a bit." Fortunately Jimmy French did arrive with a box of attractive nametags. Apparently the calligraphy effort took longer than anticipated and the next few minutes was a scene of scrambling at the check-in table as name tags were put in transparent holders, strings attached, and efforts made to find people who had already arrived. One hundred name tags not in alphabetical order on a table with people hovering around makes for an interesting picture. Given the prevalence of small cameras in the crowd the confusion was well documented.

Now that people were armed with name tags they could take a quick peek and then shake hands or hug people they hadn't seen in years. Because of the featured speaker this dinner would definitely have a basketball motif. Three seniors on that team were present, French, Greenbaum, and Grant. The other members of the team were invited, but only Eddie Gaines and Butch Stephens were present. A sigh of relief was breathed when Larry Munson did arrive shortly before dinner was served. Other members of the news media were present including the two reporters who had covered high school sports in the 1950s, Edgar Allen and Jimmy Davy. When the Nashville Banner folded Allen moved to Louisville, Kentucky to work for Churchill Downs, but at the time of the reunion both he and Davy were retired and living in the Nashville area. Allen died in 2008.

The pleasantries and visiting continued throughout the dinner and after everyone in the room introduced themselves the stage was set for the featured address. Jimmy French introduced Larry Munson going all the way back to his time as a minor league baseball announcer when most people in the audience were in grammar school or junior high. The people planning the reunion felt they had scored a real coup by getting Munson to come and speak. Even though he had not lived in Nashville, or even Tennessee, for many years there were people in the class who had continued to stay in touch with him. It was said that in all the years of broadcasting he believed the saga of the West High basketball team in 1954 was the most exciting story he had ever been a part of. When Larry began to speak the unmistakable voice carried many in the crowd back to an earlier time. Then the fun started.

For about thirty minutes he gave a rambling discourse that covered a wide range of subjects and other than questioning Jimmy French about why he shot a hook shot in the closing minutes of the LaFollette game, it rarely touched on anything relating to 1954. As the evening went on I kept waiting for him to tie it all together, but that moment never came. Reflecting on it later I gathered that Larry Munson was a play-by-play type of guy who could comment in a colorful fashion on whatever was right in front of him, but a prepared speechmaker he was not. What did we expect anyway? This was a guy who described the winning touchdown in the 2001 Georgia-Tennessee game with the words "We just stepped on their face with a hobnailed boot and broke their nose. We just crushed their face." What he had to say at the reunion dinner was not quite so memorable, but it was vintage Munson. The man spent the $200 he got with his Army discharge to go to broadcasting school in

Minnesota. For the next sixty years he thrilled audiences with his unique style. His reference to hobnailed boots puts him in select company with the Beatles (Happiness is a Warm Gun) and Harry Potter (Harry Potter and the Deathly Hallows). He certainly did his part in 1954 to make the West High "miracle" a part of Nashville history. Actually, the TSSAA had recognized the "miracle" at the state basketball tournament held earlier that year with several team members in attendance.

Munson was followed by Coach Shapiro who gave the speech we had come to hear. In his typical understated and totally factual style he acknowledged the success of his teams and gave credit to Doc and the students at West High as well as the athletes in attendance. He also acknowledged the presence of his wife Ruth who had won the title of Mrs. Tennessee in 1956. It was a memorable evening.

The next day at the school was much more informal and gave people a chance to visit with one another more than the night before. Cameras were again in abundance and many people brought scrapbooks, some going back to junior high days at Waverly-Belmont and Cavert. Some even had pictures from grammar school years at Eakin or Clemons elementary schools! There were copies of news stories as well as the Jack Knox cartoon following the championship game, but probably the most sought after information was the driving directions to the Legends Club for the cookout later that night. When we were in school there was nothing between Nashville and Franklin but farmland. In 2004 it would be easy to miss the golf course in the midst of houses and shopping centers.

The festive mood was interrupted for a memorial service in the auditorium for the 26 deceased classmates. In an unlikely assignment I was the person to moderate the event. Fortunately there were three ministers and a talented musician to carry the heavy load and all I had to do was introduce people. Gene Rutledge had picked out the music earlier and printed programs with an agenda and lyrics to the songs. Hijacking a somewhat out of tune piano from the music room enabled Joyce Tummins Byrd to play the accompaniment to Gene's selections. Rather than a sermon Fred Johnson gave a brief address. In some ways it was an uncomfortable topic because it focused on the limited remaining time we all had. It was certainly interesting to sit in a room in a building most had not been in for fifty years and recall a time when we were young and our lives and dreams were in front of us. Now our dreams have been achieved, abandoned, or altered. Fred emphasized his desire to "finish well." The big "All The Way For Doc" type dreams are there for our children and grandchildren, but the lessons learned in that saga are still with us. In an atmosphere where you could hear a pin drop the names of the deceased classmates were read by John Kepler and Wanda Whitwell Suggs. It had been years since John played the trumpet, but his career had led him to California and a number of acting jobs and commercials in addition to a career with computers. Five decades earlier Wanda was better known as Minnie Pearl for her imitation of the Grand Ole Opry comedienne, but there was no attempt at humor on this occasion. She laughingly told me that even with her now gray hair she still does the Pearl routine at nursing homes where the residents know exactly what and who she is talking about. In the unstructured part of the program class members were encouraged to share memories and stories were told. They were usually lighthearted enough to keep the mood from being totally sad. David Compton offered a closing prayer. It was a necessary part of the weekend, but I was emotionally drained when it was over. My plans to play golf at the Legends Club before the cookout were cancelled for a long nap.

Everyone found the club without any trouble and even though the event was outdoors under a covered veranda the weather was not nearly as hot and humid as you would expect in June. It was hard to believe that an event which had been in the planning stage for more than three years was coming to an end, a little over twenty four hours since it began. There were a number of door prizes. Various people felt compelled to give testimonials about what the high school experience had meant to them, but Ralph Greenbaum said it best when he said "this was about a lot more than basketball."

After a final appeal for donations the sad goodbyes were said and the usual assurances to stay in touch exchanged. No immediate plans were made for another reunion, but it was announced that a final accounting of the weekend would be calculated. A surplus was anticipated and would be donated to the school. The next spring at a luncheon of the West High Lunch Bunch a check for $2,500 was given to the principal. The money was to be used for books in the library and each book would show that it had been donated by the Class of 1954.

FINAL THOUGHTS

I am indebted to a number of people for their help and encouragement in this book, but I am primarily grateful that the Nashville Public Library has the back issues of the Banner and Tennessean on microfilm. Spending hours looking at film and putting countless quarters in the machine making copies enabled me to be as factual as possible about events described herein. I was consistently amazed at how inaccurate my memory was about a lot of events where I was an eyewitness.

I also benefitted from materials provided by Coach Shapiro's son John after the funeral in May of 2009. He had discovered the basketball scorebooks from 1949-1968 which served to supplement my research at the library. Again I was reminded that my memory of events is not always accurate and it is helpful to have access to records that were kept at the time of the events. This not only allowed for correcting errors in the early drafts of this book, but provided supplemental information I would have never known about. The scorebooks have now been entrusted to Ray Sharer so they can find a suitable place in the Alumni Room at West End Middle School. Ray, along with other faithful members of the West High Lunch Bunch, deserves special thanks for their efforts in keeping the memories of the school not only alive, but on display. It is through their efforts the school is on the registry of historic sites and Coach Shapiro has been nominated for the Tennessee and Nashville Sports Hall of Fame. Another helpful book which is unfortunately out of print now is "Those Were The Glory Years" by West High graduate (1948) Wallace Stanley Tyson.

I am also grateful that a number of other books have been written about high school basketball in the 1950s. While it is obvious I disagreed with what I thought was the hyperbolic nature of most of the books, they were nonetheless helpful in capturing the mood of the era. What was more helpful was Robert Ikard's objective and factual book on AAU women's basketball. The websites that exist for schools like Meigs (www.meigsmagnetms.mnps.org) and Cameron (www.cameronms.mnps.org) provided a lot of information about the history of those schools I could not find elsewhere. The website for the National Negro High School tournament (www.bbreunion.com) was another jewel I stumbled on as I was writing this book.

This started out to be a basketball book and in the end that is, at least in part, what it is. I knew I wanted to write a story that was more than a factual recitation of events. The goal was to write something that included a description of the time and place where the story occurred. Sometimes the atmosphere (time and place) of an event explains what happened more than any box score ever can. For example, do people remember the state tournament of 1954 more so than other tournaments? I believe they do because the circumstances that led to the "All The Way For Doc" cheer were unlike any earlier tournament. The retirement of the only principal the school had ever known and the chance to be the first school to win the championship four times was a combination sure to attract attention. The fact that the team in question was from a major city with two competitive newspapers also helped with the hype. The tournaments occurred during a slow sports news period. Other than spring training stories about the Nashville Vols baseball team there really wasn't much else to report. Does anyone remember who won the state title when West didn't in 1945, 1947, or between 1949 and 1953? They probably do not. The tournament is held every year and to be memorable there has to be something to differentiate it from other events.

This was also the first of many tournaments held at the Vanderbilt Gym. The Munson broadcasts attracted a large audience beyond the four walls of the place where the games were held. There have been many games played since before larger crowds that were also broadcast, but there is a first time character about the 1954 tournament that distinguishes it from the others. The 1965 tournament which marked the beginning of integration in Tennessee high school sports is certainly an equally great milestone event for entirely different reasons.

I knew when I began this effort there might be readers who would be disappointed if I did not characterize the effort of the West High team in 1954 as one of the greatest, if not the greatest, achievement in Tennessee high school basketball. But, I never believed it was and I knew that was not the book I intended to write.

I do believe the winning of four titles in eleven years may be the greatest single achievement of any high school in Tennessee up to that time. But, that was achieved with many different players and two dissimilar coaches. The only consistent factor was the school principal and Doc would be the first to tell you he had nothing to do with it. Was this the best West team of the four champions? I think a case can be made for that distinction. It lacked individual stars like the Lawrence brothers, George Kelley, Harry Moneypenny, Billy Joe Adcock, or Bob Dudley Smith. But, the balanced scoring and team defense may be superior to the teams of the 1940s. Certainly the level of competition was greater for this team than the earlier ones. There were a few easy games during the season and a couple in the tournaments, but for the most part it was top rank competition in practically all of the games.

A tournament is not always won by the best team, but by the team that happens to be playing the best at that time. I don't think I'm alone in my assessment, but I thought Lake City was a better team than West. Kingsport, which was eliminated in the semi finals, might have been the best team of all the sixteen schools that played in the tournament. Looking at their season records you would certainly have to say Woodlawn, Donelson, and LaFollette were every bit as good as West. The games against MBA, McEwen, and Treadwell could have been lost in the final minutes. The manner in which the Blue Jays capitalized on the mistakes of others was more important than any domination of the opposition. They did not dominate their opponents, certainly not in the manner Pearl did in 1965 and 1966, but Pearl had something to prove.

Which brings us to the question of how good was Tennessee high school basketball in the days of segregation anyway? What would this team do if they had to take a shot in 30 seconds? How many points would they score if longer jump shots counted three points? These are the types of questions and arguments that can go on forever and not be resolved. My own opinion is that even if Jimmy French couldn't kill the clock with unlimited dribbling any coach would want to have him handling the ball. Billy Owens would still be guarding the best shooter on the other team, and Ralph Greenbaum and Buddy Parsons would be making a lot of three point baskets. The concepts of teamwork and discipline are timeless, but the final answer to the question is "No, this team would probably not be competitive today."

Most of the basketball books I referred to in an earlier chapter have a lot of interviews and quotes from the coach and players. I intentionally did not do that although it would have been fairly simple to locate many of the people. The book I wanted to write was to be from my point of view and if any of the principal characters have a different point of view they are free to express it. There were some other reasons that relate to logistical difficulties. Vaughn Dubose died in 1999 and both Billy Owens and Jerry Morrison died in 2005. There were several players I went to college with (French, Greenbaum, Grant, and Gaines), as well as both managers (Christian and Lewis). Butch Stephens went to the University of Tennessee, but I saw him off and on for many years leading up to the 2004 reunion. Certainly there were conversations with those people that I relied on in putting this project together. There were others than I have not seen or talked to since 1954 (Parsons, Greer, Glenn). After high school I had some contact with Doc because of his political campaigns. While my brother and I played a round in a golf tournament one summer with Coach Shapiro, that was the only contact I recall with him after graduation besides the class reunions mentioned earlier. I am glad I had an opportunity to talk with him and his wife at a small reunion luncheon in 1998. There was such a large crowd at the 50th Reunion that I was unable to get to them. I was saddened to hear of Mrs. Shapiro's death in 2005 which I read about in the online edition of the Tennessean. When I saw the news in May 2009 of Coach Shapiro's death I knew it was time to drop everything and go to Nashville. It was a great opportunity to meet his family who I had only barely known as children. It was hardly a sad occasion because he had lived such a full life and was alert and active into his 90s. The animated conversations between former students and players at the visitation sounded more like a party than a wake.

In mathematics we are told that the total is the sum of its parts, but I think what I got out of the whole West End High School experience is far greater than that. I realize there were plenty of people who had the same exposure and it meant very little to them. How else do you explain the fact that people were willing to travel at their own expense and come to Nashville from Hawaii, California, Texas, Florida, Arizona and other states in 2004 to spend time with people they had not seen in fifty years? On the other hand there were people who lived within ten miles of the school who not only didn't attend the reunion, but never responded to any of the mailings. For them I suppose the total must be less than the sum of the same parts I was exposed to.

Lessons learned are not dependant on a favorable outcome. I am glad we beat MBA in football, but I would still have gone to law school if we lost. If Ralph Greenbaum had missed one of the free throws to put the Donelson game into overtime he would still have become a doctor. Hindsight is always interesting. In his remarks at the 50th reunion Coach Shapiro expressed more disappointment about not winning the state baseball championship in 1953 than any euphoria he felt at winning the state basketball trophy ten months later. Members of that baseball team, who were also a part of the basketball team, seem to feel the same way. I know I was surprised when I researched my own performance on the golf team and found I had played much better than I remembered. While it is easy to assume everyone who was touched by the events at West End High School in 1954 had a similar experience, there is plenty of evidence to suggest that a wide variety of reactions exist. My perspective has certainly changed over time. When I was a senior in high school I tended to look upon it as an exciting and singular event. Today I see it as a part of the many events that shaped my life and not necessarily the most important one. But, it is certainly not the least significant one either. In the end I can say that although there were many times I thought it was over (MBA, Donelson, McEwen, Lake City, Treadwell, and LaFollette), I never gave up hope and I am glad we won.

Being a part of such an experience was an excellent preparation for the rest of my life. Aiming high for realistic goals, but having to accept something less than total victory is what we all eventually face. When you're young the rest of your life is a blank slate and you can write whatever script you want. Events will fill in the blanks and the outcome is probably not going to be what you dreamed of as a teenager. But, as the James Taylor song says, "The secret of life is enjoying the passage of time." The West High saga of 1954 was very enjoyable and trying to put the experience into words has been equally so.

The author is a 1954 graduate of West End High School and a 1958 graduate of Vanderbilt University, majoring in English. He graduated from the Nashville School of Law in 1963 and practiced law in Nashville from 1963-1969. He was an attorney in Washington, DC from 1970-1978 and a faculty member at Bethune-Cookman College in Daytona Beach, Florida from 1979-1988. He has been an independent business and legal consultant since 1989 and presently lives in Louisville, Kentucky.

CPSIA information can be obtained
at www.ICGtesting.com
Printed in the USA
LVHW092159190420
654091LV00004B/34/J